Peltzer · Scesniak

Wertpapierhandelsgesetz/German Securities Trade Act

D1719678

German Securities Trade Act

German-English Text
with an Introduction in English

by

Dr. Martin Peltzer
Attorney-at-law and Notar, Frankfurt am Main

Paul Scesniak
Attorney-at-law, Frankfurt am Main

Verlag
Dr. Otto Schmidt
Köln

Wertpapierhandelsgesetz

Deutsch-englische Textausgabe
mit einer englischen Einleitung

von

Dr. Martin Peltzer
Rechtsanwalt und Notar, Frankfurt am Main

Paul Scesniak
Attorney-at-law, Frankfurt am Main

Verlag
Dr. Otto Schmidt
Köln

Die Deutsche Bibliothek – CIP-Einheitsaufnahme

German securities trade act: German-English text with an introduction in English / by Martin Peltzer; Paul Scesniak. – Köln: O. Schmidt, 1995
Parallelt.: Wertpapierhandelsgesetz

ISBN 3-504-40060-9

NE: Peltzer, Martin [Hrsg.]; Wertpapierhandelsgesetz

Verlag Dr. Otto Schmidt KG
Postfach 51 10 26, 50946 Köln
Tel.: 02 21/9 37 38-01, Fax: 02 21/9 37 38-9 21

Satz: Lichtsatz Heinrich Fanslau, Düsseldorf
Druck und Verarbeitung: Bercker Graphischer Betrieb GmbH, Kevelaer

Printed in Germany

Vorwort

Mit dem Inkrafttreten des Wertpapierhandelsgesetzes ist in Deutschland eine seit langem bestehende Gesetzeslücke geschlossen worden. In den meisten Ländern mit einem hochentwickelten Kapitalmarkt bestehen seit Jahren wirksame Vorschriften gegen den Mißbrauch von Insiderinformationen – ein Mißbrauch, der regelmäßig Fairneß gegenüber anderen Marktteilnehmern verletzt. Die bisher bestehenden Regelungen auf freiwilliger Grundlage haben sich letztlich als zu schwach erwiesen, und zudem war Deutschland gezwungen, die EU-Insiderhandelsrichtlinie in deutsches Recht umzusetzen. Deutschland hat also, was die Bekämpfung von Insidermißbräuchen angeht, nunmehr endlich den internationalen Standard erreicht.

Wertpapiermärkte leben von Informationen: Diese Informationen dürfen nicht durch Insider mißbraucht werden; darüber hinaus müssen sie möglichst schnell und geordnet den Marktteilnehmern zugänglich sein. Dementsprechend legt das neue Gesetz den Emittenten von Wertpapieren entsprechende Mitteilungspflichten auf. Schließlich befaßt sich das Gesetz weiter mit den Pflichten von Wertpapierdienstleistern, also in erster Linie Banken, gegenüber Wertpapierkunden und den Meldepflichten von Marktteilnehmern, die Aktienpakete an börsennotierten Unternehmen kaufen und verkaufen.

Verstöße gegen das neue Wertpapierhandelsgesetz können außerordentlich schwerwiegende Folgen haben. Das Gesetz droht hierfür Freiheits- und Geldstrafe sowie hohe Geldbußen an. Betroffen sein kann jeder, der sich als Anleger, Bank, verantwortlicher Unternehmensleiter eines Emittenten, Paketkäufer oder in sonstiger Eigenschaft mit Wertpapieren befaßt. Da auch zahlreiche Marktteilnehmer, die nicht genügend Deutsch sprechen, das Gesetz zu beachten haben, legen wir eine synoptisch deutsch-englische Fassung mit einer Einleitung in Englisch vor.

Frankfurt, im Herbst 1994   Martin Peltzer
                                                              Paul Scesniak

Foreword

The Security Trade Act's coming into force closes a long-standing legal gap in Germany. Effective regulations against the misuse of insider information – misuse that regularly infringes upon fairness to other market participants – have existed in most countries with highly developed capital markets for years. Heretofore existing voluntary regulations ultimately proved themselves too weak and, additionally, Germany was forced to implement EU Insider Trading Guidelines in German law. Thus, Germany has now finally reached the international standard as far as fighting insider misuse is concerned.

Securities markets live on information: Insiders may not misuse this information. Furthermore, the information has to be made accessible to market participants as quickly as possible and in an ordered manner. Accordingly, the new Act imposes appropriate reporting duties upon the issuer of securities. Lastly, the Act concerns itself further with duties of securities services providers; that is, primarily with banks' duties to their securities customers and with reporting duties of market participants who buy and sell blocks of shares in exchange-quoted enterprises.

Violations of the new Securities Trade Act can have extraordinarily serious consequences. The Act threatens with prison terms, monetary criminal penalties and high administrative fines for violations. Anyone can be affected who has to do with securities as an investor, bank, responsible executive of an issuer, block buyer or in another capacity. Because many market participants who are subject to the Act do not speak sufficient German to understand the Act's text, we are providing a synoptic German-English version with an introduction in English.

Frankfurt, Autumn 1994

Martin Peltzer
Paul Scesniak

Inhaltsverzeichnis/Contents

The Securities Trade Act – a Survey

I. Prologue

It seems to have taken longer in Germany than in other countries for the belief to establish itself that information – after all, an essential ingredient of securities trading – should be made accessible as quickly as possible and simultaneously to all participants in the securities market. It violates fundamental fairness to allow insiders, because of better information, to participate in securities trading, to sell securities facing bad news and to buy securities facing good news if the other market participants do not share such information. By the same token, important information has to be quickly disseminated so that all market participants can adjust for it.

This was not at all accepted everywhere in Germany even as late as in the 1960s and the exploitation of insider knowledge was, in the main, customary. Only at the end of the 1960s did the realization set in that in a world becoming smaller and smaller, rules would have to be introduced similar to those long since prevailing in other countries with organized stock exchanges. The first insider trading guidelines were passed in 1970, then revised in 1976 and again in 1988. These were not yet generally valid rules, but rather a voluntary code of behaviour to which one had to expressly subject oneself. In the case of most companies quoted on the stock exchange, however, acknowledging insider trading guidelines was demanded of the executive and supervisory board members. In any case, the procedure, compared to provisions in other countries, was not particularly effective. In the early days of insider trading guidelines, there were a couple of dozen proceedings of which only one is still remembered. The AEG supervisory board chairman bought company stock before it was generally known that Daimler-Benz would acquire a majority holding. He had to surrender his gains of DM 16,000.

In the meantime, European legal development has forced the Federal Republic to take action against insider misuse with more potent means. The Council issued the Insider Guideline (Guideline 89/592/EEC of November 17, 1989) on November 13, 1989, which member states were to implement in national law before June 1, 1992. The Federal Republic was two years late in meeting this obligation. The Securities Trade Act which implemented the guideline went or shall come into effect only on August 1, 1994 or January 1, 1995. Additionally, the Securities Trade Act implements an additional guideline, namely the Transparency Guideline (Council Guideline 88/627 EEC of December 12, 1988). The Transparency Guideline was to have already been implemented by January 1, 1991.

II. Insider securities

The definition of insider securities stems from §§ 2 and 12. First of all, § 2 defines the Act's general securities concept. Accordingly, securities are stocks, certificates representing stocks (e.g. interim certificates and global documents), bonds, profit-sharing certificates (which can contain a wide spectrum of rights), option certificates (which generally certify the right to buy stocks at a fixed price) and other securities "comparable to stocks and bonds". An additional identifying characteristic of the securities concept is marketability in a market according to the definition of § 2 para. 1. According to § 2 para. 2, derivatives are rights whose exchange or market price is a function of the exchange or market price of securities within the meaning of para. 1 or of the exchange or market price of foreign currencies or of changes in interest rates. Derivatives had to be included in the Act – at least to the extent that they are related to securities – because, after all, their prices relate directly to the prices of securities and so, just as more directly in the case of securities, the danger of insider trading misuse is present.

After the definition of securities found in § 2, § 12 defines the concept of insider securities which is at once narrower and broader. For example, according to § 12 para. 1, all insider securities are securities but not all securities are insider securities. For example, such securities as are handled neither on an exchange nor in over-the-counter trading are not insider securities even if they could be traded there without further ado. On the other hand, the concept of insider securities is also broader than the concept of securities because, according to § 12 para. 2 nos. 2 to 4, it also embraces derivatives, independently defined in § 2, and which precisely are not securities within the meaning of the Act.

III. The insider

The Act distinguishes between the primary insider (§ 13 para. 1) and the secondary insider (§ 14 para. 2).

There are three groups of primary insiders (§ 13 para. 1), namely;

– the member of a corporate body of the issuer or of an enterprise affiliated with the issuer, that is, in the normal case of a stock corporation, a member of the executive or supervisory board. But because, additionally, non-stock companies can also issue insider securities (e.g. profit-sharing certificates) or because an affiliated enterprise can also be a limited liability company or a limited partnership, insider within this group can also be a managing director of a limited liability company or personally liable partner of either a limited or general partnership (the born insider),

– a shareholder; that is, normally a stockholder of the issuer, who due to his shareholding obtains insider intelligence, or

– whoever gains knowledge of insider facts in the proper performance of his

profession, employment or task. CPAs, tax advisors, attorneys and, for example, even employees of the issuer or of an affiliated enterprise are contemplated here.

The definition of the born insider (§ 13 para. 1 no. 2) is simple. In the case of equity holding pursuant to § 13 para. 1 no. 2, it is not a matter of the extent of the holding although it certainly would be the exception if a small shareholder learned of insider facts "on the basis of" his equity holding in the issuer or in an affiliated enterprise (that is, causally). In the case of the third group (no. 3), knowledge of the insider fact has to be acquired in "proper performance", coincidental knowledge does not count. The difference can be seen in an example. If the acquirer in a planned take-over commissions a CPA to analyse the balance sheet of the target company, then the CPA is a primary insider. If the same CPA (without having been commissioned by the acquirer) happens to overhear a conversation in which the acquisition is the topic, then he has not acquired knowledge in "proper performance" and is a secondary insider.

A secondary insider can be anyone who coincidentally attains knowledge of an insider fact. The textbook examples are the taxi driver who listens to a conversation of his customers or a stewardess who coincidentally hears snippets of passenger conversation or – a case from American legal practice – a psychiatrist to whom a frustrated patient recounts that her husband intends to change over to another company.

IV. The bar to insider trading and its implementation by means of threatened criminal penalties

A primary insider is subject to a three-way bar at the outset (§ 14).

a. He may neither acquire nor sell securities "by exploitation" of his insider knowledge and indeed neither for his own nor for someone else's account nor for someone else. It is irrelevant here whether the insider gains personal advantage or not. So, for example, the executor of a will or asset manager may not make use of his insider knowledge. This may very well lead him into conflicts of interest, but that will not stay the bar.

b. He may not unauthorisedly report or make an insider fact accessible to someone else. Authorized passing on of insider facts is not barred, therefore passing on information to the Federal Supervisory Agency in the context of reporting duties or reporting to other authorities on the basis of public law duties (e.g. reporting the emission of poisonous materials to the environmental protection authorities, although this can certainly be an insider fact because of the resulting damage restitution claims against the enterprise) or also passing on insider facts to employees professionally engaged therewith in an investment bank.

c. He may not recommend the sale or the acquisition of securities to someone else on the basis of his own insider knowledge. In this variation, the insider fact in itself is not passed on 0 in assets.

3

Simply abstaining on the basis of insider knowledge is not barred. Whoever therefore intended to acquire or sell a particular security but then refrained from doing this because of his insider knowledge does not violate the bar. This provision takes account of practical reason, because such abstention on the basis of insider knowledge could practically never be proven.

Only a part of this list is barred to a secondary insider. He is just as restricted as the primary insider regarding exploitation of coincidentally acquired insider knowledge, that is, he is barred from acquiring or selling securities as is the primary insider according to IV. a above.

The bar to insider trading is implemented with the help of criminal law. Whoever violates an applicable bar as either primary or secondary insider risks a monetary or jail penalty of up to five years. The length of such threatened prison term – in comparison to threatened penalties in the case of property torts – leads to the realization of how seriously the legislature views insider violations. Violating a corresponding foreign bar is deemed to be the equal of violating § 14's bar to insider trading.

V. Other measures for bringing about equality of opportunity in securities trading

1. Publication of price-influencing facts (§ 15)

As determined above, news is an essential element of securities market trading. The real topic of the Securities Trade Act is therefore how to treat news, the misuse of which is not only to be prevented – precisely by the bars to insider trading – but which is really supposed to be disseminated as quickly as possible in order to give all securities market participants an equal chance.

Accordingly, every issuer of securities admitted to trading on a domestic exchange must publicise a new fact which has come to be known in his sphere of activity and which is not publically known if such fact is capable of substantially influencing the exchange price of the admitted securities because of the fact's effects on the financial and asset situation of the issuer or on the general course of business of the issuer. In the event that the issuer's securities are bonds which can, after all, also be issued by an issuer whose stocks are not traded on the exchange or whose legal form of business does not allow the issuer to enter the exchange with its own securities, it is a question of whether its ability to perform its duties arising out of these bonds can be detrimentally affected by the underlying facts.

The provision creates a number of difficult questions and it can be assumed that they will occupy both practice and academia.

First of all, it always has to be a matter of facts and therefore not rumours or opinions. But a fact can also very well exist in a company decision such as buying another company or splitting off from a group company or, in the

case of a pharmaceutical enterprise, bringing a revolutionary new medicine onto the market, etc. In such cases, however, the question arises as to how far along the company decision must be. As a rule, the issuer is a stock corporation with a supervisory board responsible for approving such decisions. The issuer, however, will hardly be able to make a report pursuant to § 15 without having earlier obtained the consent of the supervisory board on the matter which, in turn, means that the matter – the fact necessitating the report – will have reached a considerable degree of finality and in a borderline case will have been known to the issuer for a long time. Up to 20 and in the case of a steel and coal industry co-determined supervisory board up to 21 members of the supervisory board shall have to have been sent documents concerning the matter before the supervisory board meeting at which the matter is scheduled to be decided and share owners and union representatives will often have had colleagues review such documents, so that the circle of the informed parties, that is, secret-bearers, at this stage before reporting pursuant to § 15 is quite large and the danger of an insider violation grows.

The fact must be "capable" of "substantially" influencing the exchange price. First of all, this means that the representatives of the issuer must be able to anticipatorily recognise that this fact by itself can substantially influence the price. Other influencing factors such as interest rate changes, generally good or bad economic or political news are, therefore, not to be considered, or are to be subtracted out to some extent. Failing to report pursuant to § 15 can result in considerable monetary penalties in misdemeanour proceedings which, in turn, can be subjected to judicial review if a concerned party wants to defend itself against the monetary penalty.

The substantiality of the influence on the exchange price depends on whether the market of the security in question is broad or narrow. A stock which has a very narrow market will naturally be easier to drive upwards or downwards than a stock that has a broad market. To this extent no fixed limits (X %) recommend themselves for informing the fact characteristic "substantially".

Only facts are to be reported which are "not publicly known". Of course, it is in the interest of the issuer to obviate this fact characteristic immediately by making the fact known – by reporting to newspapers, news agencies etc. – so that § 15 would amount to nothing or would be limited to the cases in which the issuer, pursuant to § 15 para. 1 last sentence, wants to arrive at the result that the fact does not have to be publicised. So the question resolves itself into a consideration of whether the form and order of § 15 is to be maintained or whether a price-relevant fact can simply be publicised with the result that § 15, then, would no longer be applicable precisely because the fact, in the meantime, had become known. According to § 15 para. 3 sentence 2 one probably has to assume that, in the case of facts within the meaning of para. 1, § 15 necessarily applies. This also makes sense because the prioritised informing of the exchanges assures that trading in the

affected security will be temporarily suspended and no one will be able to suffer damages or gain advantage because of ignorance or knowledge of the insider fact.

It has been widely considered how to limit the fact description uncertainties of § 15 in practice. It was thus suggested that an inclusive catalogue of facts be established, similar to what the SEC in the USA has done with its K 8 form, where each fact pattern triggers a duty to report; such a catalogue naturally must contain a catch-all clause because, after all, not all relevant real-life fact situations can be set out. It can be expected that the Federal Supervisory Agency, advised by business associations, will also make such a catalogue available to the practice.

§ 15 para. 6 has special meaning. The provision clearly states that infringement of reporting duties does not, in itself, trigger damage restitution claims. This should prevent small stockholders from making extortionist claims against the company if the company has not performed its public law duties pursuant to § 15.

2. Reporting duties concerning reaching, exceeding and falling below voting rights threshold values for exchange-quoted stock corporations

If § 15 concerns itself with the form and order of publicizing price-influencing facts, § 21 obliges everyone reaching or exceeding a certain voting rights threshold value for an exchange-quoted company or unrestricted hereby to inform the issuer and the Federal Supervisory Agency. The issuer, for its part, is then obliged to inform the public (§ 25). §§ 21ff implement EU Commission Transparency Guideline in German law. Reports pursuant to § 21 have substantial meaning for the market and its participants because such reports allow conclusions to be drawn concerning further price development. Krupp would have to have paid a substantially higher price in its acquisition of a majority in Hoesch or would not even have been able to reach this majority if such regulation had existed then because the intended take-over would have been recognised much earlier and the market and probably the target company, too, would have reacted much earlier. § 21 should thus prevent a raider's creeping-up, that is a creeping take-over and therefore simultaneously belongs to acquisition law. (The 13th EC Guideline is concerned with take-overs and has not yet emerged from its draft stage – not least of which because the member states can not agree that an offer to buy all stocks should be made upon reaching a threshold value of 30 %.)

The threshold values correspond respectively to certain minority or majority rights pursuant to German law. The owner of 25 % of the voting rights can prevent by-law changes and, in general, capital increases. By exceeding 50 %, the voting rights owner can implement routine decisions in a stock corporation. With over 75 %, the voting rights owner in general can determine all important structural decisions – including passing a resolution for

a control agreement. It must be born in mind here that these threshold values relate to percentage rates based, in turn, on issued voting rights capital, while in a shareholders' meeting at which certain questions are to be decided, the basis for reaching a majority or a minority is always the capital represented in such shareholders' meeting. In the case of German exchange-quoted stock corporations, this is generally not more than 70% or 80% of the issued voting rights capital and often much less than that. The reason for this is basically that particularly foreign stockholders spare themselves the expense associated with having their stocks represented at the shareholders' meeting. Votes pursuant to § 22 are attributed to the owned votes of the party under the duty to report.

Whoever does not perform his duties to report may not vote with the concerned stocks – his voting right is suspended (§ 28) – and he can be assessed a monetary penalty. Whether or not these sanctions will suffice to deter a raider intending a creeping take-over from his plan has to be considered an unanswered question.

VI. Rules of conduct for securities firms

The behavioural duties listed in § 31 now regulate statutorily that which, in a well-conducted securities firm, probably has been obvious for a long time and which in most cases really has been so – namely that the interest of the customer always comes first, that conflicts of interest are to be avoided and that an effective means for preventing conflicts of interest exists in permitting only directly involved employees access to sensitive information and to take care, by use of Chinese walls, that such information remains limited to a narrow circle.

According to § 31's general rules of conduct, securities services are to be performed with the requisite care and conscientiousness in the interest of the customer and conflicts of interest are to be avoided, or in the case of unavoidable conflicts of interest, the interests of the customer are to be appropriately preserved. Furthermore, the securities firm has a certain duty of care to the customer in that the firm has to inform itself pursuant to § 31 para. 2 to avoid that, for example, an inexperienced customer seeking a safe investment for his modest savings is sold highly speculative securities. In respect to such firm, the special rules of § 32 are to prevent that conflicts of interest are resolved to the detriment of the customer. The behavioural duties are manifested in appropriate organisational, recording and record-keeping duties pursuant to §§ 33 and 34 which are supposed to facilitate observance of duties or, in the event of non-observance, facilitate proving the violation of duty. An infringement of recording and record-keeping duties can also draw monetary penalties but an infringement of general or special conduct duties can not. The large banks have already – to an extent years ago – begun to develop compliance departments and to concern themselves with this topic. The Securities Trade Act has therefore

not caught them unprepared and they will probably have no serious difficulties with its implementation.

VII. The Federal Securities Trade Supervisory Agency and the organization of supervision

The Federal Securities Trade Supervisory Agency shall be the independent federal supreme authority within the competence of the Federal Finance Minister (§ 3) and will initially have 97 job positions. In addition to supervision of insider violations, the new Agency will also be responsible for supervision of the ad hoc duty to file reports (§ 15), supervision of reporting and information duties upon reaching, exceeding and falling below certain threshold values of voting rights capital of an exchange-quoted company, observance of compliance rules and co-operation with other authorities in the area of securities trading.

A Securities Advisory Board shall be established at the Federal Supervisory Agency and the 16 Länder [states] shall each delegate one representative (§ 5). Representatives of various specialized federal ministries, of the Bundesbank and of the Federal Banking Supervisory Agency can participate in meetings of the Securities Advisory Board. The Securities Advisory Board has an advisory function. It remains to be seen whether it will only reflect compromise achieved between the federal and state levels and gain only minuscule practical meaning.

Furthermore, supervisory organization·is extremely complicated. It embraces five levels of authority (Securities Advisory Board, Federal Supervisory Agency, stock exchange supervising authorities, trade supervising offices and stock exchange management) which in turn runs counter to the goal of deregulation.

Distinctions must be drawn regarding information that the Federal Supervisory Agency receives. According to § 9, every domestically domiciled credit institution, every branch of a foreign bank and every other enterprise admitted to participate in trade on a domestic exchange must report each transaction in securities or derivatives to the Federal Supervisory Agency "if they close the transaction in conjunction with a securities service or for their own account" (§ 9 paras. 1 and 2 specify the details on this point). Sixty to 70 million reports a year are expected with expenses for the banking industry as a whole to reach 9-digit figures.

One thing is sure; the Federal Supervisory Agency will thus have information on all securities transactions and can – and shall pursuant to § 16 para. 2 as soon as important insider information turns up and if, in the days and weeks before, trading volume has swelled – investigate such increased trading volume and, especially regarding larger orders pursuant to § 16 para. 2, demand that the credit institutions etc. under a duty to report pursuant to § 9 disclose the order giver's identity. What seems to be an Orwellian vision

for some has been for others abroad obvious practice for a long time. The spectacular successes of the SEC with insider violations in the 1980s are inconceivable without that kind of dragnet investigation. The Federal Supervisory Agency can demand documents of the credit institutions, branches of foreign banks and enterprises under a duty to give information and can enter their business offices.

However, regarding issuers and insiders, the Federal Supervisory Agency can demand information only in accordance with the criminal procedure principal that no one need incriminate himself and should be, to this extent, reminded of his right to remain silent. Additionally, this measure already implements Article 20 of the Securities Services EC Guideline. Member states are to have passed the implementing statutory and administrative provisions by July 1, 1995 and they are to have come into effect at the latest by December 31, 1995.

Gesetz über den Wertpapierhandel

vom 26. Juli 1994

Securities Trade Act

of July 26, 1994

Abschnitt 1: Anwendungsbereich, Begriffsbestimmungen

§ 1 Anwendungsbereich

Dieses Gesetz ist anzuwenden auf den börslichen und außerbörslichen Handel mit Wertpapieren und Derivaten sowie auf Veränderungen der Stimmrechtsanteile von Aktionären an börsennotierten Gesellschaften.

§ 2 Begriffsbestimmungen

(1) Wertpapiere im Sinne dieses Gesetzes sind, auch wenn für sie keine Urkunden ausgestellt sind,

1. Aktien, Zertifikate, die Aktien vertreten, Schuldverschreibungen, Genußscheine, Optionsscheine,

2. andere Wertpapiere, die mit Aktien oder Schuldverschreibungen vergleichbar sind,

wenn sie auf einem Markt gehandelt werden können, der von staatlich anerkannten Stellen geregelt und überwacht wird, regelmäßig stattfindet und für das Publikum unmittelbar oder mittelbar zugänglich ist.

(2) Derivate im Sinne dieses Gesetzes sind an einem inländischen oder ausländischen Markt im Sinne des Absatzes 1 gehandelte Rechte, deren Börsen- oder Marktpreis unmittelbar oder mittelbar von der Entwicklung des Börsen- oder Marktpreises von Wertpapieren oder ausländischen Zahlungsmitteln oder der Veränderung von Zinssätzen abhängt.

Part one: Scope of Application, Definitions

§ 1 Scope of Application

This Act applies to stock exchange and non-stock exchange trading in securities and derivatives, and to changes in voting rights shares of stockholders in exchange-quoted companies.

§ 2 Definitions

(1) Within the meaning of this Act, even if no documents are produced for them, securities are

1. stocks, certificates representing stocks, bonds, profit-sharing certificates, option certificates,

2. other securities comparable to stocks or bonds,

when they can be traded in a market regulated and supervised by governmentally recognized offices and which market regularly operates and is directly or indirectly accessible to the public.

(2) Derivatives within the meaning of this Act are rights traded on a domestic or foreign market within the meaning of para. 1 and whose stock exchange or market price directly or indirectly depends on the development of the stock exchange or market price of securities or on foreign means of payment or on change in interest rates.

(3) Wertpapierdienstleistungen im Sinne dieses Gesetzes sind

1. die Anschaffung und die Veräußerung von Wertpapieren oder Derivaten für andere,

2. die Anschaffung und die Veräußerung von Wertpapieren oder Derivaten im Wege des Eigenhandels für andere,

3. die Vermittlung von Geschäften über die Anschaffung und die Veräußerung von Wertpapieren oder Derivaten,

wenn der Umfang der Dienstleistungen einen in kaufmännischer Weise eingerichteten Geschäftsbetrieb erfordert.

(4) Wertpapierdienstleistungsunternehmen sind

1. Kreditinstitute mit Sitz im Inland sowie Zweigstellen von Unternehmen im Sinne des § 53 Abs. 1 Satz 1 und des § 53 b Abs. 1 Satz 1 des Gesetzes über das Kreditwesen oder von Unternehmen, die aufgrund einer Rechtsverordnung gemäß § 53 c des Gesetzes über das Kreditwesen gleichgestellt oder freigestellt sind,

2. andere Unternehmen mit Sitz im Inland, die an einer inländischen Börse zur Teilnahme am Handel zugelassen sind,

die Wertpapierdienstleistungen erbringen.

Abschnitt 2: Bundesaufsichtsamt für den Wertpapierhandel

§ 3 Organisation

(1) Das Bundesaufsichtsamt für den Wertpapierhandel (Bundesaufsichts-

(3) Within the meaning of this Act, securities services are

1. the acquisition and sale of securities or derivatives for others,

2. the acquisition and sale of securities or derivatives in one's own name for others,

3. the brokerage of transactions concerning the acquisition and the sale of securities or derivatives,

if the extent of the services requires a business establishment equipped in a businesslike manner.

(4) Securities firms are

1. credit institutions domiciled domestically and branches of enterprises within the meaning of § 53 para. 1 sentence 1 and § 53b para. 1 sentence 1 of the Banking Act or of enterprises which, based on an administrative rule pursuant to § 53c of the Banking Act, are deemed to be equal or are exempted,

2. other enterprises domiciled domestically which are admitted to trading on a domestic stock exchange

and which provide securities services.

Part two: Federal Securities Trade Supervisory Agency

§ 3 Organization

(1) The Federal Securities Trade Supervisory Agency (Federal Super-

amt) wird als eine selbständige Bundesoberbehörde im Geschäftsbereich des Bundesministeriums der Finanzen errichtet.

(2) Der Präsident des Bundesaufsichtsamtes wird auf Vorschlag der Bundesregierung durch den Bundespräsidenten ernannt. Die Bundesregierung hat bei ihrem Vorschlag die für das Börsenwesen zuständigen Fachministerien der Länder anzuhören.

§ 4 Aufgaben

(1) Das Bundesaufsichtsamt übt die Aufsicht nach den Vorschriften dieses Gesetzes aus. Es hat im Rahmen der ihm zugewiesenen Aufgaben Mißständen entgegenzuwirken, welche die ordnungsmäßige Durchführung des Wertpapierhandels beeinträchtigen oder erhebliche Nachteile für den Wertpapiermarkt bewirken können. Das Bundesaufsichtsamt kann Anordnungen treffen, die geeignet sind, diese Mißstände zu beseitigen oder zu verhindern.

(2) Das Bundesaufsichtsamt nimmt die ihm nach diesem Gesetz zugewiesenen Aufgaben und Befugnisse nur im öffentlichen Interesse wahr.

§ 5 Wertpapierrat

(1) Beim Bundesaufsichtsamt wird ein Wertpapierrat gebildet. Er besteht aus Vertretern der Länder. Die Mitgliedschaft ist nicht personengebunden. Jedes Land entsendet einen Vertreter. An den Sitzungen können Vertreter der Bundesministerien der Finanzen, der Justiz und für Wirtschaft,

visory Agency) shall be established as an independent federal supreme authority within the competence of the Federal Finance Ministry.

(2) The Federal President shall appoint the President of the Federal Supervisory Agency upon recommendation of the Federal Administration. The Federal Administration shall hear the specialized ministries of the states [Länder] responsible for stock exchanges in making its recommendation.

§ 4 Tasks

(1) The Federal Supervisory Agency shall supervise pursuant to the provisions of this Act. Within the framework of the tasks assigned to it, the agency shall counteract undesirable states of affairs which operate to the detriment of an orderly operation of securities trade or which can result in significant disadvantages for the securities market. The Federal Supervisory Agency can issue administrative orders which are suitable for the relief or prevention of such undesirable states of affairs.

(2) The Federal Supervisory Agency shall perform the tasks and exercise the powers assigned and granted to it pursuant to this Act exclusively in the public interest.

§ 5 Securities Advisory Board

(1) A Securities Advisory Board shall be established at the Federal Supervisory Agency. It consists of representatives of the states [Länder]. Membership is not limited to specific individuals. Each state [Land] shall delegate one representative. Representatives of the Federal Finance Ministry, the Fed-

der Deutschen Bundesbank und des Bundesaufsichtsamtes für das Kreditwesen teilnehmen. Der Wertpapierrat kann Sachverständige insbesondere aus dem Bereich der Börsen, der Marktteilnehmer, der Wirtschaft und der Wissenschaft anhören. Der Wertpapierrat gibt sich eine Geschäftsordnung.

(2) Der Wertpapierrat wirkt bei der Aufsicht mit. Er berät das Bundesaufsichtsamt, insbesondere

1. bei dem Erlaß von Rechtsverordnungen und der Aufstellung von Richtlinien für die Aufsichtstätigkeit des Bundesaufsichtsamtes,

2. hinsichtlich der Auswirkungen von Aufsichtsfragen auf die Börsen- und Marktstrukturen sowie den Wettbewerb im Wertpapierhandel,

3. bei der Abgrenzung von Zuständigkeiten zwischen dem Bundesaufsichtsamt und den Börsenaufsichtsbehörden sowie bei Fragen der Zusammenarbeit.

Der Wertpapierrat kann beim Bundesaufsichtsamt Vorschläge zur allgemeinen Weiterentwicklung der Aufsichtspraxis einbringen. Das Bundesaufsichtsamt berichtet dem Wertpapierrat mindestens einmal jährlich über die Aufsichtstätigkeit, die Weiterentwicklung der Aufsichtspraxis sowie über die internationale Zusammenarbeit.

(3) Der Wertpapierrat wird mindestens einmal jährlich vom Präsidenten des Bundesaufsichtsamtes einberufen. Er ist ferner auf Verlangen von einem Drittel seiner Mitglieder ein-

eral Justice Ministry, the Federal Economics Ministry, the German Bundesbank and the Federal Banking Supervisory Agency can participate in meetings. The Securities Advisory Board can hear experts especially from stock exchanges, market participants, from business and from academia. The Securities Advisory Board shall issue rules of order for itself.

(2) The Securities Advisory Board shall participate in supervision. The Advisory Board advises the Federal Supervisory Agency especially

1. regarding the issuance of administrative orders and establishing guidelines for supervisory activity of the Federal Supervisory Agency,

2. regarding the effects of supervisory questions on stock exchange structures, market structures and on competition in securities trading,

3. regarding delimiting authority as between the Federal Supervisory Agency and the stock exchange supervising authorities and regarding questions of cooperation.

The Securities Advisory Board can submit suggestions to the Federal Supervisory Agency concerning overall further development of practical supervision. The Federal Supervisory Agency reports to the Securities Advisory Board at least once yearly as to supervisory activities, further development of supervision practice and international cooperation.

(3) The President of the Federal Supervisory Agency shall convene the Securities Advisory Board at least once yearly. The Commission shall additionally be convened upon the

zuberufen. Jedes Mitglied hat das Recht, Beratungsvorschläge einzubringen.

§ 6 Zusammenarbeit mit Aufsichtsbehörden im Inland

(1) Das Bundesaufsichtsamt kann sich bei der Durchführung seiner Aufgaben anderer Personen und Einrichtungen bedienen.

(2) Die Börsenaufsichtsbehörden werden im Wege der Organleihe für das Bundesaufsichtsamt bei der Durchführung von eilbedürftigen Maßnahmen für die Überwachung der Verbote von Insidergeschäften nach § 14 an den ihrer Aufsicht unterliegenden Börsen tätig. Das Nähere regelt ein Verwaltungsabkommen zwischen dem Bund und den börsenaufsichtsführenden Ländern.

(3) Das Bundesaufsichtsamt für das Kreditwesen, das Bundesaufsichtsamt für das Versicherungswesen, die Deutsche Bundesbank, soweit sie die Beobachtungen und Feststellungen im Rahmen ihrer Tätigkeit nach Maßgabe des Gesetzes über das Kreditwesen macht, die Börsenaufsichtsbehörden sowie das Bundesaufsichtsamt haben einander Beobachtungen und Feststellungen mitzuteilen, die für die Erfüllung ihrer Aufgaben erforderlich sind.

§ 7 Zusammenarbeit mit zuständigen Stellen im Ausland

(1) Dem Bundesaufsichtsamt obliegt die Zusammenarbeit mit den für die Überwachung von Börsen oder anderen Wertpapiermärkten und den Wertpapierhandel zuständigen Stellen an-

demand of one third of its members. Each member has the right to submit consultative suggestions.

§ 6 Cooperation with Domestic Supervising Authorities

(1) The Federal Supervisory Agency can avail itself of other persons and institutions in the execution of its tasks.

(2) In stock exchanges subject to their supervision, the stock exchange supervising authorities shall lend use of their organs to act on behalf of the Federal Supervisory Agency in the case of the enforcement of urgent measures for supervising the bars to insider transactions pursuant to § 14. An administrative agreement between the federal government and those states [Länder] which maintain stock exchange supervision shall regulate the particulars.

(3) The Federal Banking Supervisory Agency, the Federal Insurance Supervisory Agency, the German Bundesbank to the extent that it makes observations and determinations as to the banking industry within the context of its activity pursuant to the measure of the Federal Banking Act, the stock exchange supervising authorities and the Federal Supervisory Agency shall report observations and determinations to each other as are necessary for the performance of their tasks.

§ 7 Cooperation with the Responsible Foreign Offices

(1) The Federal Supervisory Agency shall cooperate with the offices of other countries responsible for supervision of stock exchanges or of other securities markets and securities

derer Staaten. Die Vorschriften des Börsengesetzes und des Verkaufsprospektgesetzes über die Zusammenarbeit der Zulassungsstelle der Börse mit entsprechenden Stellen anderer Staaten bleiben hiervon unberührt.

(2) Das Bundesaufsichtsamt darf im Rahmen der Zusammenarbeit mit den in Absatz 1 Satz 1 genannten Stellen Tatsachen übermitteln, die für die Überwachung von Börsen oder anderen Wertpapiermärkten, des Wertpapierhandels, von Kreditinstituten, Finanzinstituten oder Versicherungsunternehmen oder damit zusammenhängender Verwaltungs- oder Gerichtsverfahren erforderlich sind. Bei der Übermittlung von Tatsachen hat das Bundesaufsichtsamt den Zweck zu bestimmen, für den diese Tatsachen verwendet werden dürfen. Der Empfänger ist darauf hinzuweisen, daß die übermittelten Tatsachen einschließlich personenbezogener Daten nur zu dem Zweck verarbeitet oder benutzt werden dürfen, zu dessen Erfüllung sie übermittelt wurden. Eine Übermittlung personenbezogener Daten unterbleibt, soweit Grund zu der Annahme besteht, daß durch sie gegen den Zweck eines deutschen Gesetzes verstoßen wird. Die Übermittlung unterbleibt außerdem, wenn durch sie schutzwürdige Interessen des Betroffenen beeinträchtigt würden, insbesondere wenn im Empfängerland ein angemessener Datenschutzstandard nicht gewährleistet wäre.

(3) Werden dem Bundesaufsichtsamt von einer Stelle eines anderen Staates Tatsachen mitgeteilt, so dürfen diese nur unter Beachtung der Zweckbestimmung durch diese Stelle offenbart oder verwertet werden.

trading. Stock Exchange Act and Sales Prospect Act regulations concerning cooperation of the stock exchange admissions office with corresponding offices of other countries shall remain unaffected hereby.

(2) Within the context of cooperation with the offices named in para. 1 sentence 1, the Federal Supervisory Agency may communicate facts necessary for the supervision of stock exchanges or of other securities markets, of securities trading, of credit institutions, of financial institutions or insurance companies or for administrative or court proceedings related hereto. In communicating facts, the Federal Supervisory Agency shall determine the purpose for which these facts may be used. The recipient shall be advised that communicated facts including information pertaining to specific individuals may be processed or used only for that purpose for which they were communicated. Information pertaining to specific individuals shall not be communicated to the extent that there is reason to assume that the purpose of a German law would be violated thereby. Communication shall also then not be undertaken when interests worthy of protection of the concerned party would be infringed by such communication, especially if an appropriate personal privacy standard is not assured in the recipient country.

(3) If the Federal Supervisory Agency is informed by an office of another country of facts, then such facts may be revealed or used only in compliance with such office's determination of purpose.

(4) Die Regelungen über die internationale Rechtshilfe in Strafsachen bleiben unberührt.

(4) Regulations concerning international legal assistance in criminal matters remain unaffected.

§ 8 Verschwiegenheitspflicht

(1) Die beim Bundesaufsichtsamt Beschäftigten und die nach § 6 Abs. 1 beauftragten Personen dürfen die ihnen bei ihrer Tätigkeit bekanntgewordenen Tatsachen, deren Geheimhaltung im Interesse eines nach diesem Gesetz Verpflichteten oder eines Dritten liegt, insbesondere Geschäfts- und Betriebsgeheimnisse sowie personenbezogene Daten, nicht unbefugt offenbaren oder verwerten, auch wenn sie nicht mehr im Dienst sind oder ihre Tätigkeit beendet ist. Dies gilt auch für andere Personen, die durch dienstliche Berichterstattung Kenntnis von den in Satz 1 bezeichneten Tatsachen erhalten. Ein unbefugtes Offenbaren oder Verwerten im Sinne des Satzes 1 liegt insbesondere nicht vor, wenn Tatsachen weitergegeben werden an

1. Strafverfolgungsbehörden oder für Straf- und Bußgeldsachen zuständige Gerichte,

2. kraft Gesetzes oder im öffentlichen Auftrag mit der Überwachung von Börsen oder anderen Wertpapiermärkten, des Wertpapierhandels, von Kreditinstituten, Finanzinstituten oder Versicherungsunternehmen betraute Stellen sowie von diesen beauftragte Personen,

soweit diese Stellen die Informationen zur Erfüllung ihrer Aufgaben benötigen. Für die bei diesen Stellen beschäftigten Personen gilt die Verschwiegenheitspflicht nach Satz 1

§ 8 Duty of Confidentiality

(1) Employees of, and pursuant to § 6 (1) persons retained by, the Federal Supervisory Agency may not unauthorizedly reveal or use facts which have become known to them because of their employment and whose confidentiality is in the interest of a party bound by this Act or of a third party, especially business and company secrets and information pertaining to specific individuals, also then when such employee or person is no longer employed or after his or her activity has ended. This applies also to other persons who have received knowledge of the facts described in sentence 1 by employment-related reporting. An unauthorized revealing or use within the meaning of sentence 1 has, in particular, not occurred if facts are further communicated to

1. criminal law enforcement authorities or to courts responsible for criminal and monetary penalty matters,

2. offices entrusted, either by operation of law or by delegation of authority, with the supervision of stock exchanges or of other securities markets, of securities trading, of credit institutions, of finance institutions or insurance companies and to persons delegated by such offices,

to the extent that such offices require the information for the performance of their tasks. The duty of confidentiality pursuant to sentence 1 applies correspondingly to the persons em-

entsprechend. An eine Stelle eines anderen Staates dürfen die Tatsachen nur weitergegeben werden, wenn diese Stelle und die von ihr beauftragten Personen einer dem Satz 1 entsprechenden Verschwiegenheitspflicht unterliegen.

(2) Die Vorschriften der §§ 93, 97, 105 Abs. 1, § 111 Abs. 5 in Verbindung mit § 105 Abs. 1 sowie § 116 Abs. 1 der Abgabenordnung gelten nicht für die in Absatz 1 Satz 1 oder 2 bezeichneten Personen, soweit sie zur Durchführung dieses Gesetzes tätig werden. Sie finden Anwendung, soweit die Finanzbehörden die Kenntnisse für die Durchführung eines Verfahrens wegen einer Steuerstraftat sowie eines damit zusammenhängenden Besteuerungsverfahrens benötigen, an deren Verfolgung ein zwingendes öffentliches Interesse besteht, und nicht Tatsachen betroffen sind, die den in Absatz 1 Satz 1 oder 2 bezeichneten Personen durch eine Stelle eines anderen Staates im Sinne von Absatz 1 Satz 3 Nr. 2 oder durch von dieser Stelle beauftragte Personen mitgeteilt worden sind.

§ 9 Meldepflichten

(1) Kreditinstitute mit Sitz im Inland, Zweigstellen von Unternehmen im Sinne des § 53 Abs. 1 Satz 1 und des § 53 b Abs. 1 Satz 1 des Gesetzes über das Kreditwesen oder von aufgrund einer Rechtsverordnung gemäß § 53 c des Gesetzes über das Kreditwesen gleichgestellten oder freigestellten Unternehmen sowie andere Unternehmen, die ihren Sitz im Inland haben und an einer inländischen Börse zur Teilnahme am Handel zugelassen sind, sind verpflichtet, dem Bundesaufsichtsamt jedes Geschäft in Wert-

ployed with such offices. Facts may be passed on to an office of another country only if such office and the persons employed by it are subject to a duty of confidentiality corresponding to sentence 1.

(2) The provisions of §§ 93, 97, 105 para. 1, § 111 para. 5 in conjunction with § 105 para. 1 and § 116 para. 1 of the Tax Code do not apply to the persons described in para. 1 sentence 1 or 2 to the extent that such persons serve to enforce this Act. The provisions shall be applied to the extent that the tax authorities require the knowledge to conduct a procedure in conjunction with a criminal tax act or a procedure to impose tax in conjunction therewith, the prosecution of which is urgently necessary in the public interest and facts are not concerned which were reported by an office of another country within the meaning of para. 1 sentence 3 no. 2, or by persons employed by such office, to persons described in para. 1. sentence 1 or 2.

§ 9 Reporting Duties

(1) Domestically domiciled credit institutions, branches of enterprises within the meaning of § 53 para. 1 sentence 1 and § 53b para. 1 sentence 1 of the Banking Act or enterprises deemed, because of an administrative rule pursuant to § 53c of the Banking Act, equal or exempt as well as other enterprises domiciled domestically and admitted to participate in trading on a domestic stock exchange are obliged to report to the Federal Supervisory Agency each transaction in securities or derivatives admitted to

papieren oder Derivaten, die zum Handel an einem Markt im Sinne des § 2 Abs. 1 in einem Mitgliedstaat der Europäischen Gemeinschaften oder in einem anderen Vertragsstaat des Abkommens über den Europäischen Wirtschaftsraum zugelassen oder in den Freiverkehr einer inländischen Börse einbezogen sind, spätestens an dem auf den Tag des Geschäftsabschlusses folgenden Werktag, der kein Samstag ist, mitzuteilen, wenn sie das Geschäft im Zusammenhang mit einer Wertpapierdienstleistung oder als Eigengeschäft abschließen. Die Verpflichtung nach Satz 1 gilt auch für Geschäfte in Aktien und Optionsscheinen, bei denen ein Antrag auf Zulassung zum Handel an einem Markt im Sinne des § 2 Abs. 1 oder auf Einbeziehung in den Freiverkehr gestellt oder öffentlich angekündigt ist. Die Verpflichtung nach den Sätzen 1 und 2 gilt auch für Unternehmen, die ihren Sitz im Ausland haben und an einer inländischen Börse zur Teilnahme am Handel zugelassen sind, hinsichtlich der von ihnen an einer inländischen Börse oder im Freiverkehr im Zusammenhang mit einer Wertpapierdienstleistung oder als Eigengeschäft geschlossenen Geschäfte.

(2) Die Mitteilung hat auf Datenträgern oder im Wege der elektronischen Datenfernübertragung zu erfolgen. Sie muß für jedes Geschäft die folgenden Angaben enthalten:

1. Bezeichnung des Wertpapiers oder Derivats und Wertpapierkennnummer,

2. Datum und Uhrzeit des Abschlusses oder der maßgeblichen Kursfeststellung,

3. Kurs, Stückzahl, Nennbetrag der Wertpapiere oder Derivate,

trading on a stock exchange within the meaning of § 2 para. 1 in a member state of the European Communities or in another contracting state to the European Economic Area Agreement or included in the over-the-counter trading of a domestic stock exchange, at the latest on the workday following the day the transaction is closed, which following workday is not a Saturday, if they close the transaction in conjunction with a securities service or for their own account. The obligation pursuant to sentence 1 applies also to transactions in stocks and option certificates concerning which an application for admission to trade on a market within the meaning of § 2 para. 1 or to inclusion in over-the-counter trading has been submitted or publicly announced. The obligation pursuant to sentences 1 and 2 applies also to enterprises domiciled abroad and admitted to participate in trade to a domestic stock exchange regarding the transactions which they close on a domestic stock exchange or in over-the-counter trading in conjunction with a securities service or for their own account.

(2) Reporting of facts shall take place by data media or by remote electronic data transmission. The report must include the following information for each transaction:

1. name of the security or derivative and securities identifying number,

2. date and time of day of closing or of the relevant price fixing,

3. price, quantity, nominal amount of the securities or derivatives,

4. die an dem Geschäft beteiligten Kreditinstitute, Zweigstellen und Unternehmen im Sinne des Absatzes 1,

5. die Börse oder das elektronische Handelssystem der Börse, sofern es sich um ein Börsengeschäft handelt,

6. Kennzeichen zur Identifikation des Geschäfts.

Geschäfte für eigene Rechnung sind gesondert zu kennzeichnen.

(3) Das Bundesministerium der Finanzen kann durch Rechtsverordnung, die nicht der Zustimmung des Bundesrates bedarf,

1. nähere Bestimmungen über Inhalt, Art, Umfang und Form der Mitteilung und über die zulässigen Datenträger und Übertragungswege erlassen,

2. zusätzliche Angaben vorschreiben, soweit diese zur Erfüllung der Aufsichtsaufgaben des Bundesaufsichtsamtes erforderlich sind,

3. zulassen, daß die Mitteilungen der Verpflichteten auf deren Kosten durch die Börse oder einen geeigneten Dritten erfolgen, und die Einzelheiten hierzu festlegen,

4. für Geschäfte, die Schuldverschreibungen oder bestimmte Arten von Derivaten zum Gegenstand haben, zulassen, daß Angaben nach Absatz 2 nicht oder in einer zusammengefaßten Form mitgeteilt werden,

5. die in Absatz 1 genannten Kreditinstitute, Zweigstellen und Unternehmen von der Mitteilungspflicht nach Absatz 1 für Geschäfte befreien, die an einem Markt im

---

4. credit institutions, branches and enterprises within the meaning of para. 1 participating in the transaction,

5. the stock exchange or the electronic trading system of the stock exchange to the extent that it is a stock exchange transaction,

6. mark for identification of the transaction.

Transactions for one's own account are to be identified separately.

(3) The Federal Finance Ministry can, by administrative rule which does not require the consent of the Federal Senate,

1. issue additional regulations concerning content, type, extent and form of the report and concerning the permissible data media and transmission routes,

2. prescribe additional information to the extent that this is necessary for the performance of supervisory tasks of the Federal Supervisory Agency,

3. allow that the obligated parties' reports be performed at their costs through the stock exchange or through an appropriate third party and determine the details hereto,

4. allow that information pursuant to para. 2 shall not be or shall be in summarized form reported for transactions having as their objects bonds or particular types of derivatives,

5. exempt credit institutions, branches, and enterprises named in para. 1 from the duty to report pursuant to para. 1 regarding transactions executed in a market

Sinne des § 2 Abs. 1 in einem anderen Mitgliedstaat der Europäischen Gemeinschaften oder in einem anderen Vertragsstaat des Abkommens über den Europäischen Wirtschaftsraum abgeschlossen werden, wenn in diesem Staat eine Mitteilungspflicht mit gleichwertigen Anforderungen besteht,

6. bei Sparkassen und Kreditgenossenschaften, die sich zur Ausführung des Geschäfts einer Girozentrale oder einer genossenschaftlichen Zentralbank oder des Zentralkreditinstituts bedienen, zulassen, daß die in Absatz 1 vorgeschriebenen Mitteilungen durch die Girozentrale oder die genossenschaftliche Zentralbank oder das Zentralkreditinstitut erfolgen, wenn und soweit der mit den Mitteilungspflichten verfolgte Zweck dadurch nicht beeinträchtigt wird.

(4) Das Bundesministerium der Finanzen kann die Ermächtigung nach Absatz 3 durch Rechtsverordnung auf das Bundesaufsichtsamt übertragen.

§ 10 Zwangsmittel

Das Bundesaufsichtsamt kann seine Verfügungen, die es innerhalb seiner gesetzlichen Befugnisse trifft, mit Zwangsmitteln nach den Bestimmungen des Verwaltungs-Vollstreckungsgesetzes durchsetzen. Es kann auch Zwangsmittel gegen juristische Personen des öffentlichen Rechts anwenden. Die Höhe des Zwangsgeldes beträgt abweichend von § 11 des Verwaltungs-Vollstreckungsgesetzes bis zu 50 000 Deutsche Mark.

within the meaning of § 2 para. 1 in another member state of the European Communities or in another contracting state of the European Economic Area Agreement if a duty to report with substantially equivalent requirements exists in such country,

6. in the case of savings and loans and credit co-operatives which make use of a clearing house or of a co-operative central bank or of the central credit institution in order to execute the transaction, allow that the reports prescribed in para. 1 shall be performed by the clearing house or by the co-operative central bank or by the central credit institution, if and to the extent that the purpose contemplated by the duties to inform is not thereby infringed upon.

(4) The Federal Finance Ministry can delegate the authority pursuant to para. 3 by administrative rule to the Federal Supervisory Agency.

§ 10 Enforcement Means

The Federal Supervisory Agency can enforce its orders issued within its statutory powers with enforcement means pursuant to the provisions of the Administration Enforcement Act. The Agency can also apply enforcement means against public law legal entities. The coercive payment shall be up to 50,000 German Marks, at variance from § 11 of the Administration Enforcement Act.

§ 11 Kosten

(1) Die Kosten des Bundesaufsichtsamtes sind dem Bund zu erstatten

1. zu 75 Prozent durch Kreditinstitute mit Sitz im Inland und Zweigstellen von Unternehmen im Sinne des § 53 Abs. 1 Satz 1 und des § 53 b Abs. 1 Satz 1 des Gesetzes über das Kreditwesen oder von Unternehmen, die aufgrund einer Rechtsverordnung gemäß § 53 c des Gesetzes über das Kreditwesen gleichgestellt oder freigestellt sind, sofern diese Kreditinstitute oder Zweigstellen das Effektengeschäft im Inland betreiben dürfen,

2. zu 5 Prozent durch die Kursmakler, Freimakler und andere zur Teilnahme am Börsenhandel zugelassene Unternehmen, die nicht unter Nummer 1 fallen,

3. zu 10 Prozent durch Emittenten mit Sitz im Inland, deren Wertpapiere an einer inländischen Börse zum Handel zugelassen oder mit ihrer Zustimmung in den Freiverkehr einbezogen sind.

In den Fällen der Nummern 1 und 2 werden die Kosten nach Maßgabe des Umfangs der Geschäfte in Wertpapieren und Derivaten anteilig umgelegt. Im Fall der Nummer 3 werden die Kosten auf die Emittenten nach Maßgabe der Börsenumsätze ihrer zum Handel zugelassenen oder in den Freiverkehr einbezogenen Wertpapiere anteilig umgelegt.

(2) Die nach Absatz 1 Satz 1 Verpflichteten und die inländischen Börsen haben dem Bundesaufsichtsamt auf Verlangen Auskünfte über den Geschäftsumfang und die Börsenumsät-

§ 11 Costs

(1) Costs of the Federal Supervisory Agency shall be reimbursed to the Federal Government

1. 75 percent by domestically domiciled credit institutions and branches of enterprises within the meaning of § 53 para. 1 sentence 1 and § 53b para. 1 sentence 1 of the Banking Act or by enterprises deemed to be the equal thereof or exempted on the basis of an administrative rule pursuant to § 53c of the Banking Act to the extent that such credit institutions or branches may domestically conduct commissionable securities business,

2. 5 percent by exchange brokers, free brokers and other enterprises admitted to participate in stock exchange trading not included under no. 1,

3. 10 percent by issuers domiciled domestically whose securities are admitted to a domestic stock exchange for trading or are included with their consent in over-the-counter trading.

As regards nos. 1 and 2, costs shall be shared proportionately in accordance with the extent of the transactions in securities and derivatives. As regards no. 3, costs shall be shared proportionately by the issuers in accordance with the stock exchange turnovers of their securities admitted to trading or included in over-the-counter trading.

(2) Domestic stock exchanges and parties obliged pursuant to para. 1 sentence 1 must inform the Federal Supervisory Agency upon demand as to the extent of transactions and stock

ze zu erteilen. Die Kostenforderungen werden vom Bundesaufsichtsamt nach den Vorschriften des Verwaltungs-Vollstreckungsgesetzes durchgesetzt.

(3) Das Nähere über die Erhebung der Umlage nach Absatz 1 und über die Beitreibung bestimmt das Bundesministerium der Finanzen durch Rechtsverordnung, die nicht der Zustimmung des Bundesrates bedarf; es kann in der Rechtsverordnung Mindestbeträge festsetzen. Das Bundesministerium der Finanzen kann die Ermächtigung durch Rechtsverordnung auf das Bundesaufsichtsamt übertragen.

(4) Die Kosten, die dem Bund durch die Prüfung nach § 36 Abs. 1 entstehen, sind von den betroffenen Unternehmen gesondert zu erstatten und auf Verlangen des Bundesaufsichtsamtes vorzuschießen.

exchange turnovers. The Federal Supervisory Agency shall enforce the cost demands pursuant to the regulations of the Administration Enforcement Act.

(3) The Federal Finance Ministry shall determine additional particulars as to cost-sharing pursuant to para. 1 and regarding collection by administrative rule which does not require the consent of the Federal Senate; the Ministry can establish minimum amounts in the administrative rule. The Federal Finance Ministry can delegate the authority by administrative rule to the Federal Supervisory Agency.

(4) Costs which accrue to the Federal Government through audit pursuant to § 36 para. 1 shall be separately reimbursed by the concerned enterprises and, upon demand of the Federal Supervisory Agency, in advance.

Abschnitt 3:
Insiderüberwachung

§ 12 Insiderpapiere

(1) Insiderpapiere sind Wertpapiere, die

1. an einer inländischen Börse zum Handel zugelassen oder in den Freiverkehr einbezogen sind, oder

2. in einem anderen Mitgliedstaat der Europäischen Gemeinschaften oder einem anderen Vertragsstaat des Abkommens über den Europäischen Wirtschaftsraum zum Handel an einem Markt im Sinne des § 2 Abs. 1 zugelassen sind.

Der Zulassung zum Handel an einem Markt im Sinne von § 2 Abs. 1 oder der Einbeziehung in den Freiver-

Part three:
Insider Supervision

§ 12 Insider Securities

(1) Insider securities are securities which

1. are admitted to trading on a domestic stock exchange or included in over-the-counter trading or

2. are admitted within the meaning of § 2 para. 1 to trading on a stock exchange within another member state of the European Communities or in another contracting state to the European Economic Area Agreement.

Admission to trading in a market within the meaning of § 2 para. 1 or inclusion in over-the-counter trading

kehr steht gleich, wenn der Antrag auf Zulassung oder Einbeziehung gestellt oder öffentlich angekündigt ist.

(2) Als Insiderpapiere gelten auch

1. Rechte auf Zeichnung, Erwerb oder Veräußerung von Wertpapieren,

2. Rechte auf Zahlung eines Differenzbetrages, der sich an der Wertentwicklung von Wertpapieren bemißt,

3. Terminkontrakte auf einen Aktien- oder Rentenindex oder Zinsterminkontrakte (Finanzterminkontrakte) sowie Rechte auf Zeichnung, Erwerb oder Veräußerung von Finanzterminkontrakten, sofern die Finanzterminkontrakte Wertpapiere zum Gegenstand haben oder sich auf einen Index beziehen, in den Wertpapiere einbezogen sind,

4. sonstige Terminkontrakte, die zum Erwerb oder zur Veräußerung von Wertpapieren verpflichten,

wenn die Rechte oder Terminkontrakte in einem Mitgliedstaat der Europäischen Gemeinschaften oder einem anderen Vertragsstaat des Abkommens über den Europäischen Wirtschaftsraum zum Handel an einem Markt im Sinne des § 2 Abs. 1 zugelassen oder in den Freiverkehr einbezogen sind und die in den Nummern 1 bis 4 genannten Wertpapiere in einem Mitgliedstaat des Abkommens über den Europäischen Wirtschaftsraum zum Handel an einem Markt im Sinne des § 2 Abs. 1 zugelassen oder in den Freiverkehr einbezogen sind. Der Zulassung der Rechte oder Terminkontrakte zum Handel an einem

are equivalent when the application for admission or inclusion has been submitted or publicly announced.

(2) The following are also deemed to be insider securities:

1. rights to subscription, acquisition or sale of securities,

2. rights to payment of a remainder amount measured by securities' value development,

3. futures contracts on a stock or bond index or payment date contracts (financial futures contracts) and rights to subscription, acquisition or sale of finance futures contracts to the extent that the finance futures contracts have securities as objects or relate to an index in which securities are included,

4. other futures contracts which create a duty to acquire or sell securities,

if the rights or futures contracts are admitted to trading in a market within the meaning of § 2 para. 1 or included in the over-the-counter trading of a member state of the European Communities or in another contracting state to the European Economic Area Agreement, and the securities named in nos. 1 to 4 are admitted to trading in a market within the meaning of § 2 para. 1 in a member state of the European Economic Area Agreement or are included in over-the-counter trading. The admission of the rights or futures contracts to trading in a market within the meaning of § 2 para. 1 or their inclusion in over-the-

Markt im Sinne des § 2 Abs. 1 oder ihrer Einbeziehung in den Freiverkehr steht gleich, wenn der Antrag auf Zulassung oder Einbeziehung gestellt oder öffentlich angekündigt ist.

counter trading is equivalent if the application for admission or inclusion has been submitted or publicly announced.

§ 13 Insider

(1) Insider ist, wer

1. als Mitglied des Geschäftsführungs- oder Aufsichtsorgans oder als persönlich haftender Gesellschafter des Emittenten oder eines mit dem Emittenten verbundenen Unternehmens,

2. aufgrund seiner Beteiligung am Kapital des Emittenten oder eines mit dem Emittenten verbundenen Unternehmens oder

3. aufgrund seines Berufs oder seiner Tätigkeit oder seiner Aufgabe bestimmungsgemäß

Kenntnis von einer nicht öffentlich bekannten Tatsache hat, die sich auf einen oder mehrere Emittenten von Insiderpapieren oder auf Insiderpapiere bezieht und die geeignet ist, im Falle ihres öffentlichen Bekanntwerdens den Kurs der Insiderpapiere erheblich zu beeinflussen (Insidertatsache).

(2) Eine Bewertung, die ausschließlich aufgrund öffentlich bekannter Tatsachen erstellt wird, ist keine Insidertatsache, selbst wenn sie den Kurs von Insiderpapieren erheblich beeinflussen kann.

§ 13 Insider

(1) An insider is whoever

1. as member of the management or supervisory body or as personally liable shareholder of the issuer or of an enterprise affiliated with the issuer,

2. on the basis of his or her equity holding in the capital of the issuer or of an enterprise affiliated with the issuer or

3. on the basis of the proper performance of his or her occupation, employment or task,

has knowledge of a fact not publicly known relating to one or more issuers of insider securities or to insider securities and which fact is capable of substantially influencing the price of the insider securities in the event of it becoming publicly known (insider fact).

(2) An appraisal which is produced exclusively on the basis of publicly known facts is no insider fact even if such appraisal can substantially influence the price of insider securities.

§ 14 Verbot von Insidergeschäften

(1) Einem Insider ist es verboten,

1. unter Ausnutzung seiner Kenntnis von einer Insidertatsache Insiderpapiere für eigene oder fremde

§ 14 Bar to Insider Transactions

(1) An insider is barred from

1. acquiring or selling insider securities for his or her own account or for the account of others or for

Rechnung oder für einen anderen zu erwerben oder zu veräußern,

2. einem anderen eine Insidertatsache unbefugt mitzuteilen oder zugänglich zu machen,

3. einem anderen auf der Grundlage seiner Kenntnis von einer Insidertatsache den Erwerb oder die Veräußerung von Insiderpapieren zu empfehlen.

(2) Einem Dritten, der Kenntnis von einer Insidertatsache hat, ist es verboten, unter Ausnutzung dieser Kenntnis Insiderpapiere für eigene oder fremde Rechnung oder für einen anderen zu erwerben oder zu veräußern.

§ 15 Veröffentlichung und Mitteilung kursbeeinflussender Tatsachen

(1) Der Emittent von Wertpapieren, die zum Handel an einer inländischen Börse zugelassen sind, muß unverzüglich eine neue Tatsache veröffentlichen, die in seinem Tätigkeitsbereich eingetreten und nicht öffentlich bekannt ist, wenn sie wegen der Auswirkungen auf die Vermögens- und Finanzlage oder auf den allgemeinen Geschäftsverlauf des Emittenten geeignet ist, den Börsenpreis der zugelassenen Wertpapiere erheblich zu beeinflussen, oder im Fall zugelassener Schuldverschreibungen die Fähigkeit des Emittenten, seinen Verpflichtungen nachzukommen, beeinträchtigen kann. Das Bundesaufsichtsamt kann den Emittenten auf Antrag von der Veröffentlichungspflicht befreien, wenn die Veröffentlichung der Tatsache geeignet ist, den berechtigten Interessen des Emittenten zu schaden.

another by exploitation of his knowledge of an insider fact,

2. reporting or making accessible an insider fact to another without proper authorization,

3. recommending the acquisition or the sale of insider securities to another on the basis of his knowledge of an insider fact.

(2) A third party with knowledge of an insider fact is barred from acquiring or selling insider securities for his own account or for the account of others or for another by exploitation of such knowledge.

§ 15 Publication and Reporting of Price-influencing Facts

(1) The issuer of securities admitted to trading on a domestic stock exchange must without delay publicize a new fact which has arisen in the issuer's sphere of activity and which is not publicly known if such fact is capable, because of its effects on the asset and financial situation or general course of business of the issuer of substantially affecting the stock exchange price of the admitted securities or, in the case of admitted bonds, if such fact can act to the detriment of the issuer's ability to satisfy his obligations. The Federal Supervisory Agency can exempt the issuer upon application from the duty to publicize if publication of the fact is capable of damaging the justified interests of the issuer.

(2) Der Emittent hat die nach Absatz 1 zu veröffentlichende Tatsache vor der Veröffentlichung

1. der Geschäftsführung der Börsen, an denen die Wertpapiere zum Handel zugelassen sind,

2. der Geschäftsführung der Börsen, an denen ausschließlich Derivate im Sinne des § 2 Abs. 2 gehandelt werden, sofern die Wertpapiere Gegenstand der Derivate sind, und

3. dem Bundesaufsichtsamt

mitzuteilen. Die Geschäftsführung darf die ihr nach Satz 1 mitgeteilte Tatsache vor der Veröffentlichung nur zum Zwecke der Entscheidung verwenden, ob die Feststellung des Börsenpreises auszusetzen oder einzustellen ist.

(3) Die Veröffentlichung nach Absatz 1 Satz 1 ist

1. in mindestens einem überregionalen Börsenpflichtblatt oder

2. über ein elektronisch betriebenes Informationsverbreitungssystem, das bei Kreditinstituten, Zweigstellen von Unternehmen im Sinne des § 53 Abs. 1 Satz 1 und des § 53b Abs. 1 Satz 1 des Gesetzes über das Kreditwesen, anderen Unternehmen, die ihren Sitz im Inland haben und an einer inländischen Börse zur Teilnahme am Handel zugelassen sind, und Versicherungsunternehmen weit verbreitet ist,

in deutscher Sprache vorzunehmen. Eine Veröffentlichung in anderer Weise darf nicht vor der Veröffentlichung nach Satz 1 erfolgen. Im Bundesanzeiger ist unverzüglich ein Hinweis auf die Veröffentlichung nach Satz 1 bekanntzumachen. Das Bundesaufsichtsamt kann bei umfangreichen Angaben gestatten, daß eine Zusam-

(2) The issuer shall report the fact to be publicized pursuant to para. 1 before such publication to

1. the management of the stock exchanges on which the securities are admitted to trading,

2. the management of the stock exchanges on which exclusively derivatives within the meaning of § 2 para. 2 are traded to the extent that the securities are the object of the derivatives and

3. the Federal Supervisory Agency.

Management may make use of the fact reported to it pursuant to sentence 1 before publication only in order to decide whether fixing of the stock exchange price shall be suspended or discontinued.

(3) Publication, pursuant to para. 1 sentence 1, is,

1. in at least one national stock exchange official notice journal or

2. through an electronically driven information dissemination system which is commonly found in credit institutions, branches of enterprises within the meaning of § 53 para. 1 sentence 1 and § 53b para. 1 sentence 1 of the Banking Act, in other domestically domiciled enterprises admitted to participate in trading on a domestic stock exchange and in insurance companies,

to be performed in the German language. Publication in another manner may not take place before the publication pursuant to sentence 1. A reference to publication pursuant to sentence 1 shall be made in the Federal Gazette without delay. The Federal Supervisory Agency can allow, in the case of voluminous information, that

menfassung gemäß Satz 1 veröffentlicht wird, wenn die vollständigen Angaben bei den Zahlstellen des Emittenten kostenfrei erhältlich sind und in der Veröffentlichung hierauf hingewiesen wird; Satz 3 gilt hierfür entsprechend.

(4) Der Emittent hat die Veröffentlichung nach Absatz 3 Satz 1 unverzüglich der Geschäftsführung der in Absatz 2 Satz 1 Nr. 1 und 2 erfaßten Börsen und dem Bundesaufsichtsamt zu übersenden.

(5) Das Bundesaufsichtsamt kann von dem Emittenten Auskünfte und die Vorlage von Unterlagen verlangen, soweit dies zur Überwachung der Einhaltung der in den Absätzen 1 bis 4 geregelten Pflichten erforderlich ist. Während der üblichen Arbeitszeit ist seinen Bediensteten und den von ihm beauftragten Personen, soweit dies zur Wahrnehmung seiner Aufgaben erforderlich ist, das Betreten der Grundstücke und Geschäftsräume des Emittenten zu gestatten. § 16 Abs. 6 und 7 gilt entsprechend.

(6) Verstößt der Emittent gegen die Verpflichtung nach Absatz 1, 2 oder 3, so ist er einem anderen nicht zum Ersatz des daraus entstehenden Schadens verpflichtet. Schadensersatzansprüche, die auf anderen Rechtsgrundlagen beruhen, bleiben unberührt.

§ 16 Laufende Überwachung

(1) Das Bundesaufsichtsamt überwacht das börsliche und außerbörsliche Geschäft in Insiderpapieren, um Verstößen gegen die Verbote nach § 14 entgegenzuwirken.

(2) Hat das Bundesaufsichtsamt Anhaltspunkte für einen Verstoß gegen ein Verbot nach § 14, so kann es von

a summary be publicized pursuant to sentence 1 if complete information is available at no cost at the paying agents of the issuer and reference is made hereto in the publication; sentence 3 applies hereto respectively.

(4) The issuer shall send the publication pursuant to para. 3 sentence 1 without delay to the management of the stock exchanges indicated in para. 2 sentence 1 nos. 1 and 2 and to the Federal Supervisory Agency.

(5) The Federal Supervisory Agency can demand information of the issuer and the submission of documents to the extent that this is necessary for supervising the performance of the duties regulated in paras. 1 to 4. Entrance upon the real estate and into the offices of the issuer shall be granted to the Agency's employees and to its delegated persons during normal working hours to the extent that this is necessary for the performance of the Agency's duties. § 16 paras. 6 and 7 apply respectively.

(6) If the issuer violates his duty pursuant to para. 1, 2 or 3, then he is not liable for restitution of damages resulting therefrom to another. Damage restitution claims based on other legal grounds are hereby unaffected.

§ 16 Continuous Supervision

(1) The Federal Supervisory Agency supervises stock exchange and nonstock exchange transactions in insider securities in order to counteract violations of the bars pursuant to § 14.

(2) If the Federal Supervisory Agency has reasons to believe that a violation of a bar pursuant to § 14 has taken

den in § 9 Abs. 1 Satz 1 genannten Kreditinstituten, Zweigstellen und Unternehmen Auskünfte über Geschäfte in Insiderpapieren verlangen, die sie für eigene oder fremde Rechnung abgeschlossen oder vermittelt haben. Das Bundesaufsichtsamt kann vom Auskunftspflichtigen die Angabe der Identität der Auftraggeber, der berechtigten oder verpflichteten Personen sowie der Bestandsveränderungen in Insiderpapieren verlangen, soweit es sich um Insiderpapiere handelt, für welche die Anhaltspunkte für einen Verstoß vorliegen oder deren Kursentwicklung von solchen Insiderpapieren abhängt.

(3) Im Rahmen der Auskunftspflicht nach Absatz 2 kann das Bundesaufsichtsamt vom Auskunftspflichtigen die Vorlage von Unterlagen verlangen. Während der üblichen Arbeitszeit ist seinen Bediensteten und den von ihm beauftragten Personen, soweit dies zur Wahrnehmung seiner Aufgaben erforderlich ist, das Betreten der Grundstücke und Geschäftsräume der in Absatz 2 Satz 1 genannten Kreditinstitute, Zweigstellen und Unternehmen zu gestatten. Das Betreten außerhalb dieser Zeit, oder wenn die Geschäftsräume sich in einer Wohnung befinden, ist ohne Einverständnis nur zur Verhütung von dringenden Gefahren für die öffentliche Sicherheit und Ordnung zulässig und insoweit zu dulden. Das Grundrecht der Unverletzlichkeit der Wohnung (Artikel 13 des Grundgesetzes) wird insoweit eingeschränkt.

(4) Hat das Bundesaufsichtsamt Anhaltspunkte für einen Verstoß gegen ein Verbot nach § 14, so kann es von

place, then the Agency can demand information regarding transactions in insider securities of the credit institutions, branches and enterprises described in § 9 para. 1 sentence 1 which have executed or brokered transactions for their own or other accounts. The Federal Supervisory Agency can demand that the party under a duty to give information report the identity of the order givers, the benefited or encumbered persons and the portfolio holdings changes in insider securities to the extent that it is a matter of insider securities regarding which there are reasons to believe a violation has taken place or whose price development depends on such insider securities.

(3) Within the context of the reporting duty pursuant to para. 2, the Federal Supervisory Agency can demand that parties under a duty to report information submit documents. Entrance upon the real estate and into the offices of credit institutions, branches and enterprises specified in para. 2 sentence 1 shall be granted to the Federal Supervisory Agency's employees and to its delegated persons during normal working hours to the extent that this is necessary for the performance of the Agency's duties. Entrance without permission and other than during such working hours or if the offices are located in living quarters is permissible, and to such extent to be tolerated, only if to prevent a present danger to public safety and order. The constitutional right of the inviolability of living quarters (Article 13 of the Constitution) is, to such extent, restricted.

(4) If the Federal Supervisory Agency has reasons to suspect a violation of a bar pursuant to § 14, then the Agency

den Emittenten von Insiderpapieren und den mit ihnen verbundenen Unternehmen, die ihren Sitz im Inland haben oder deren Wertpapiere an einer inländischen Börse zum Handel zugelassen sind, sowie den Personen, die Kenntnis von einer Insidertatsache haben, Auskünfte über Insidertatsachen und über andere Personen verlangen, die von solchen Tatsachen Kenntnis haben.

(5) Das Bundesaufsichtsamt kann von Personen, deren Identität nach Absatz 2 Satz 2 mitgeteilt worden ist, Auskünfte über diese Geschäfte verlangen.

(6) Der zur Erteilung einer Auskunft Verpflichtete kann die Auskunft auf solche Fragen verweigern, deren Beantwortung ihn selbst oder einen der in § 383 Abs. 1 Nr. 1 bis 3 der Zivilprozeßordnung bezeichneten Angehörigen der Gefahr strafgerichtlicher Verfolgung oder eines Verfahrens nach dem Gesetz über Ordnungswidrigkeiten aussetzen würde. Der Verpflichtete ist über sein Recht zur Verweigerung der Auskunft zu belehren.

(7) Widerspruch und Anfechtungsklage gegen Maßnahmen nach den Absätzen 2 bis 5 haben keine aufschiebende Wirkung.

§ 17 Verarbeitung und Nutzung personenbezogener Daten

(1) Das Bundesaufsichtsamt darf ihm nach § 16 Abs. 2 Satz 2 mitgeteilte personenbezogene Daten nur für Zwecke der Prüfung, ob ein Verstoß gegen ein Verbot nach § 14 vorliegt, und der internationalen Zusammen-

can demand of the issuers of insider securities and of their domestically domiciled affiliated enterprises or of affiliated enterprises whose securities are admitted to trading on a domestic stock exchange and of persons who have knowledge of an insider fact, information regarding insider facts and information regarding other persons who have knowledge of such facts.

(5) The Federal Supervisory Agency can demand of persons whose identity has been reported pursuant to para. 2 sentence 2 information concerning such transactions.

(6) The party under a duty to give information can refuse to give information concerning questions the answers to which could expose such party or a relative specified in § 383 para. 1 nos. 1 to 3 of the Civil Procedure Code to the danger of criminal justice prosecution or to the danger of a proceeding pursuant to the Misdemeanors Act. The party under a duty shall be informed of his right to refuse to give information.

(7) Objection to and action to set aside measures pursuant to paras. 2 to 5 have no deferring effect.

§ 17 Processing and Use of Information Pertaining to Specific Individuals

(1) The Federal Supervisory Agency may store, modify and use information pertaining to specific individuals reported to it pursuant to § 16 para. 2 sentence 2 only for purpose of reviewing whether a violation of a bar

arbeit nach Maßgabe des § 19 speichern, verändern und nutzen.

(2) Personenbezogene Daten, die für Prüfungen oder zur Erfüllung eines Auskunftsersuchens einer zuständigen Stelle eines anderen Staates nach Absatz 1 nicht mehr erforderlich sind, sind unverzüglich zu löschen.

§ 18 Strafverfahren bei Insidervergehen

(1) Das Bundesaufsichtsamt hat Tatsachen, die den Verdacht einer Straftat nach § 38 begründen, der zuständigen Staatsanwaltschaft anzuzeigen. Es kann die personenbezogenen Daten der Betroffenen, gegen die sich der Verdacht richtet oder die als Zeugen in Betracht kommen, der Staatsanwaltschaft übermitteln.

(2) Dem Bundesaufsichtsamt sind die Anklageschrift, der Antrag auf Erlaß eines Strafbefehls und der Ausgang des Verfahrens mitzuteilen, soweit dies für die Wahrnehmung seiner Aufgaben nach diesem Abschnitt erforderlich ist.

§ 19 Internationale Zusammenarbeit

(1) Das Bundesaufsichtsamt übermittelt den zuständigen Stellen anderer Mitgliedstaaten der Europäischen Gemeinschaften oder anderer Vertragsstaaten des Abkommens über den Europäischen Wirtschaftsraum die für die Überwachung der Verbote von Insidergeschäften erforderlichen Informationen. Es macht von seinen Befugnissen nach § 16 Abs. 2 bis 5 Gebrauch, soweit dies zur Erfüllung des Auskunftsersuchens der in Satz 1 genannten zuständigen Stellen erforderlich ist.

pursuant to § 14 exists and for the purpose of international cooperation pursuant to the measure of § 19.

(2) Information pertaining to specific individuals which is no longer necessary for review or fulfillment of a request for information from a responsible office of another country pursuant to para. 1 shall be deleted without delay.

§ 18 Criminal Law Proceedings upon Insider Transgressions

(1) The Federal Supervisory Agency shall refer facts which justify suspicion of a criminal act pursuant to § 38 to the responsible district attorney's office. The Agency can communicate information relating to the parties whom the suspicion concerns or who are possible witnesses to the district attorney's office.

(2) The criminal complaint, the petition for an order of summary punishment and the result of the proceedings are to be reported to the Federal Supervisory Agency to the extent that this is necessary for the performance of its tasks pursuant to this Part.

§ 19 International Cooperation

(1) The Federal Supervisory Agency shall communicate information necessary for supervising bars to insider transactions to the responsible offices of other member states of the European Communities or of other contracting states to the European Economic Area Agreement. The Agency shall make use of its powers pursuant to § 16 para. 2 to 5 to the extent that this is necessary to meet requests for information from the responsible offices specified in sentence 1.

(2) Bei der Übermittlung von Informationen sind die zuständigen Stellen im Sinne des Absatzes 1 Satz 1 darauf hinzuweisen, daß sie unbeschadet ihrer Verpflichtungen in strafrechtlichen Angelegenheiten, die Verstöße gegen Verbote von Insidergeschäften zum Gegenstand haben, die ihnen übermittelten Informationen ausschließlich zur Überwachung des Verbotes von Insidergeschäften oder im Rahmen damit zusammenhängender Verwaltungs- oder Gerichtsverfahren verwenden dürfen.

(3) Das Bundesaufsichtsamt kann die Übermittlung von Informationen verweigern, wenn

1. die Weitergabe der Informationen die Souveränität, die Sicherheit oder die öffentliche Ordnung der Bundesrepublik Deutschland beeinträchtigen könnte oder

2. aufgrund desselben Sachverhalts gegen die betreffenden Personen bereits ein gerichtliches Verfahren eingeleitet worden ist oder eine unanfechtbare Entscheidung ergangen ist.

(4) Das Bundesaufsichtsamt darf die ihm von den zuständigen Stellen im Sinne des Absatzes 1 Satz 1 übermittelten Informationen, unbeschadet seiner Verpflichtungen in strafrechtlichen Angelegenheiten, die Verstöße gegen Verbote von Insidergeschäften zum Gegenstand haben, ausschließlich für die Überwachung der Verbote von Insidergeschäften oder im Rahmen damit zusammenhängender Verwaltungs- oder Gerichtsverfahren verwenden. Eine Verwendung dieser Informationen für andere Zwecke der Überwachung nach § 7 Abs. 2 Satz 1 oder in strafrechtlichen Angelegenheiten in diesen Bereichen oder ihre

(2) In the event information is communicated, the responsible offices within the meaning of para. 1 sentence 1 are to be informed that they may use the information communicated to them, without prejudice to their duties in criminal law matters regarding violations of bars to insider transactions, exclusively for supervising the bar to insider transactions or within the context of administrative or court proceedings in conjunction therewith.

(3) The Federal Supervisory Agency can refuse to communicate information if

1. the passing on of such information could infringe upon the sovereignty, the security or the public order of the Federal Republic of Germany or

2. a court proceeding on the basis of the same fact pattern has already been begun against the concerned persons or if a non-appealable judgment has been rendered.

(4) The Federal Supervisory Agency may use the information communicated to it by the responsible offices within the meaning of para.1 sentence 1, without prejudice to its duties in criminal law matters regarding violations of the bars to insider transactions, exclusively for supervision of the bars to insider transactions or within the context of administrative or court proceedings in conjunction therewith. Use of such information for other purposes of supervision pursuant to § 7 para 2 sentence 1 or in criminal law matters in these areas or the relaying of such information to responsible offices of other countries

Weitergabe an zuständige Stellen anderer Staaten für Zwecke nach Satz 1 bedarf der Zustimmung der übermittelnden Stellen.

(5) Das Bundesaufsichtsamt kann für die Überwachung der Verbote von Insidergeschäften im Sinne des § 14 und entsprechender ausländischer Verbote mit den zuständigen Stellen anderer als der in Absatz 1 Satz 1 genannten Staaten zusammenarbeiten und diesen Stellen Informationen nach Maßgabe des § 7 Abs. 2 übermitteln. Absatz 1 Satz 2 ist entsprechend anzuwenden.

§ 20 Ausnahmen

Die Vorschriften dieses Abschnitts sind nicht auf Geschäfte anzuwenden, die aus geld- oder währungspolitischen Gründen oder im Rahmen der öffentlichen Schuldenverwaltung vom Bund, einem seiner Sondervermögen, einem Land, der Deutschen Bundesbank, einem ausländischen Staat oder dessen Zentralbank oder einer anderen mit diesen Geschäften beauftragten Organisation oder mit für deren Rechnung handelnden Personen getätigt werden.

Abschnitt 4: Mitteilungs- und Veröffentlichungspflichten bei Veränderungen des Stimmrechtsanteils an börsennotierten Gesellschaften

§ 21 Mitteilungspflichten des Meldepflichtigen

(1) Wer durch Erwerb, Veräußerung oder auf sonstige Weise 5 Prozent, 10 Prozent, 25 Prozent, 50 Prozent oder

---

for purposes pursuant to sentence 1 requires the consent of the communicating offices.

(5) The Federal Supervisory Agency can cooperate with the responsible offices of countries other than those specified in para. 1 sentence 1 for the supervision of bars to insider transactions within the meaning of § 14 and for the supervision of equivalent foreign bars and communicate information to such offices pursuant to the measure of § 7 para. 2. Para 1 sentence 2 is applicable respectively.

§ 20 Exceptions

The provisions of this Part are not to be applied to transactions performed because of fiscal or monetary policy reasons or in the context of public debt management of the Federal Government, one of its special assets, of a state [Land], of the German Bundesbank, of a foreign country or its central bank or of another organization charged with such transactions or with persons acting for their accounts.

Part four: Reporting and Publication Duties upon Changes in Voting Rights Shares in Exchange-quoted Companies

§ 21 Reporting Duties of the Party under a Duty to Report

(1) Whoever reaches, exceeds or falls below by acquisition, sale or in another manner 5 percent, 10 percent,

75 Prozent der Stimmrechte an einer börsennotierten Gesellschaft erreicht, überschreitet oder unterschreitet (Meldepflichtiger), hat der Gesellschaft sowie dem Bundesaufsichtsamt unverzüglich, spätestens innerhalb von sieben Kalendertagen, das Erreichen, Überschreiten oder Unterschreiten der genannten Schwellen sowie die Höhe seines Stimmrechtsanteils unter Angabe seiner Anschrift schriftlich mitzuteilen. Die Frist beginnt mit dem Zeitpunkt, zu dem der Meldepflichtige Kenntnis davon hat oder nach den Umständen haben mußte, daß sein Stimmrechtsanteil die genannten Schwellen erreicht, überschreitet oder unterschreitet.

(2) Börsennotierte Gesellschaften im Sinne dieses Abschnitts sind Gesellschaften mit Sitz im Inland, deren Aktien zum amtlichen Handel an einer Börse in einem Mitgliedstaat der Europäischen Gemeinschaften oder in einem anderen Vertragsstaat des Abkommens über den Europäischen Wirtschaftsraum zugelassen sind.

§ 22 Zurechnung von Stimm- rechten

(1) Für die Mitteilungspflichten nach § 21 Abs. 1 stehen den Stimmrechten des Meldepflichtigen Stimmrechte aus Aktien der börsennotierten Gesellschaft gleich,

1. die einem Dritten gehören und von diesem für Rechnung des Meldepflichtigen oder eines von dem Meldepflichtigen kontrollierten Unternehmens gehalten werden,

2. die einem Unternehmen gehören,

---

25 percent, 50 percent, or 75 percent of voting rights in a stock exchange-quoted company (party under a duty to report) shall report to the company and to the Federal Supervisory Agency without delay in writing at the latest within 7 calendar days of the reaching, exceeding or falling below the specified thresholds as well as of the amount of his voting rights share and including his address. The report notice period begins at the point in time at which the party under duty to report has knowledge thereof or should have known according to the circumstances that his voting rights share has reached, exceeded or fallen below the specified thresholds.

(2) Companies quoted on the stock exchange within the meaning of this Part are domestically domiciled companies whose stocks are admitted to official trading on a stock exchange in a member state of the European Communities or in another contracting state of the European Economic Area Agreement.

§ 22 Ascribing Voting Rights

(1) Voting rights arising from stocks of the stock exchange-quoted company are deemed to be the equivalent of voting rights of the party under a duty to report for duties to report pursuant to § 21 para. 1 if

1. the stocks belong to a third party and are kept by such third party for the account of the party under a duty to report or for the account of an enterprise controlled by the party under a duty to report,

2. the stocks belong to an enterprise

das der Meldepflichtige kontrolliert,

3. die einem Dritten gehören, mit dem der Meldepflichtige oder ein von ihm kontrolliertes Unternehmen eine Vereinbarung getroffen hat, die beide verpflichtet, langfristig gemeinschaftliche Ziele bezüglich der Geschäftsführung der börsennotierten Gesellschaft zu verfolgen, indem sie ihre Stimmrechte einvernehmlich ausüben,

4. die der Meldepflichtige einem Dritten als Sicherheit übertragen hat, es sei denn, der Dritte ist zur Ausübung der Stimmrechte aus diesen Aktien befugt und bekundet die Absicht, die Stimmrechte auszuüben,

5. an denen zugunsten des Meldepflichtigen ein Nießbrauch bestellt ist,

6. die der Meldepflichtige oder ein von ihm kontrolliertes Unternehmen durch einseitige Willenserklärung erwerben kann,

7. die dem Meldepflichtigen zur Verwahrung anvertraut sind, sofern er die Stimmrechte aus diesen Aktien nach eigenem Ermessen ausüben kann, wenn keine besonderen Weisungen des Aktionärs vorliegen.

(2) Die zuzurechnenden Stimmrechte sind in den Mitteilungen nach § 21 Abs. 1 für jede der Nummern in Absatz 1 getrennt anzugeben.

(3) Ein kontrolliertes Unternehmen ist ein Unternehmen, bei dem dem Meldepflichtigen unmittelbar oder mittelbar

1. die Mehrheit der Stimmrechte der Aktionäre oder Gesellschafter zusteht,

which the party under a duty to report controls,

3. the stocks belong to a third party with whom the party under a duty to report or an enterprise controlled by it has concluded an agreement which binds both to pursue long-term joint purposes regarding management direction of the stock exchange-quoted company in that they exercise their voting rights in unison,

4. the party under a duty to report has assigned the stocks to a third party as collateral unless such third party is authorized to exercise the voting rights arising from such stocks and announces its intention to exercise such voting rights,

5. usufruct of the stocks has been granted to the benefit of the party under a duty to report,

6. the party under a duty to report or an enterprise controlled by it can acquire the stocks by unilateral declaration,

7. the stocks have been entrusted for safekeeping to the party under a duty to report and to the extent that such party can exercise voting rights arising from such stocks in its own discretion if no special instructions of the stockholder are present.

(2) The voting rights to be ascribed are to be separately specified in the reports pursuant to § 21 para. 1 for each of the numbers in para. 1.

(3) A controlled enterprise is an enterprise for which the party under a duty to report, directly or indirectly,

1. has a right to the majority of the voting rights of the stockholders or of the shareholders,

2. als Aktionär oder Gesellschafter das Recht zusteht, die Mehrheit der Mitglieder des Verwaltungs-, Leitungs- oder Aufsichtsorgans zu bestellen oder abzuberufen, oder

3. als Aktionär oder Gesellschafter aufgrund einer mit anderen Aktionären oder Gesellschaftern dieses Unternehmens getroffenen Vereinbarung die Mehrheit der Stimmrechte allein zusteht.

§ 23 Nichtberücksichtigung von Stimmrechten

(1) Das Bundesaufsichtsamt läßt auf schriftlichen Antrag zu, daß Stimmrechte aus Aktien der börsennotierten Gesellschaft bei der Berechnung des Stimmrechtsanteils unberücksichtigt bleiben, wenn der Antragsteller

1. ein zur Teilnahme am Handel an einer Börse in einem Mitgliedstaat der Europäischen Gemeinschaften oder in einem anderen Vertragsstaat des Abkommens über den Europäischen Wirtschaftsraum zugelassenes Unternehmen ist, das Wertpapierdienstleistungen erbringt,

2. die betreffenden Aktien im Handelsbestand hält oder zu halten beabsichtigt und

3. darlegt, daß mit dem Erwerb der Aktien nicht beabsichtigt ist, auf die Geschäftsführung der Gesellschaft Einfluß zu nehmen.

(2) Das Bundesaufsichtsamt läßt auf schriftlichen Antrag eines Unternehmens mit Sitz in einem Mitgliedstaat der Europäischen Gemeinschaften oder in einem anderen Vertragsstaat des Abkommens über den Europäischen Wirtschaftsraum, das nicht die Voraussetzungen des Absatzes 1 Nr. 1

2. has the right as stockholder or shareholder to appoint or recall the majority of the members of the administrative, directing or supervisory organ or

3. has exclusive rights as stockholder or shareholder to the majority of voting rights on the basis of an agreement concluded with other stockholders or shareholders of this enterprise.

§ 23 Non-consideration of Voting Rights

(1) The Federal Supervisory Agency shall permit, upon written request, that voting rights arising from stocks of the stock exchange-quoted company shall not be considered in calculating the voting rights share if the applicant

1. is an enterprise admitted to participate in trading on a stock exchange in a member state of the European Communities or in another contracting state to the European Economic Area Agreement, which enterprise performs securities services,

2. holds or intends to hold the concerned stocks as trading stock and

3. indicates that the acquisition of the stocks is not intended to gain influence over the management direction of the company.

(2) The Federal Supervisory Agency shall permit, upon written request of an enterprise domiciled in a member state of the European Communities or in another contracting state to the European Economic Area Agreement and which enterprise does not meet the preconditions of para. 1 no. 1 that

erfüllt, zu, daß Stimmrechte aus Aktien der börsennotierten Gesellschaft für die Meldeschwelle von 5 Prozent unberücksichtigt bleiben, wenn der Antragsteller

1. die betreffenden Aktien hält oder zu halten beabsichtigt, um bestehende oder erwartete Unterschiede zwischen dem Erwerbspreis und dem Veräußerungspreis kurzfristig zu nutzen und

2. darlegt, daß mit dem Erwerb der Aktien nicht beabsichtigt ist, auf die Geschäftsführung der Gesellschaft Einfluß zu nehmen.

(3) Bei der Prüfung des Jahresabschlusses eines Unternehmens, dem gemäß Absatz 1 oder 2 eine Befreiung erteilt worden ist, hat der Abschlußprüfer in einem gesonderten Vermerk festzustellen, ob das Unternehmen die Vorschriften des Absatzes 1 Nr. 2 oder des Absatzes 2 Nr. 1 beachtet hat, und diesen Vermerk zusammen mit dem Prüfungsbericht den gesetzlichen Vertretern des Unternehmens vorzulegen. Das Unternehmen ist verpflichtet, den Vermerk des Abschlußprüfers unverzüglich dem Bundesaufsichtsamt vorzulegen. Das Bundesaufsichtsamt kann die Befreiung nach Absatz 1 oder 2 außer nach den Vorschriften des Verwaltungsverfahrensgesetzes widerrufen, wenn die Verpflichtungen nach Satz 1 oder 2 nicht erfüllt worden sind. Wird die Befreiung zurückgenommen oder widerrufen, so kann das Unternehmen einen erneuten Antrag auf Befreiung frühestens drei Jahre nach dem Wirksamwerden der Rücknahme oder des Widerrufs stellen.

(4) Stimmrechte aus Aktien, die aufgrund einer Befreiung nach Absatz 1 oder 2 unberücksichtigt bleiben, kön-

voting rights arising from stocks of the stock exchange-quoted company shall not be considered in respect of the 5 percent reporting threshold if the petitioner

1. holds or intends to hold the concerned stocks in order to make short-term use of existing or expected differences between the acquisition price and the sales price and

2. indicates that the acquisition of the stocks is not intended to exercise influence over the management direction of the company.

(3) In auditing the annual report of an enterprise which has been exempted pursuant to para. 1 or 2, the annual report auditor shall determine in a separate memorandum whether the enterprise has followed the provisions of para. 1 no. 2 or of para. 2 no. 1 and shall submit such report together with the annual report audit to the legal representatives of the enterprise. The enterprise is obliged to submit such memorandum of the annual report auditor to the Federal Supervisory Agency without delay. The Federal Supervisory Agency can repeal the exemption pursuant to para. 1 or 2 without consideration of the provisions of the Administrative Procedure Act if the duties pursuant to sentence 1 or 2 have not been met. If the exemption is rescinded or repealed, then the enterprise can apply anew for exemption at the earliest three years after the effective date of the rescission or repeal.

(4) Voting rights arising from stocks which shall not be considered because of an exemption pursuant to para. 1 or

nen nicht ausgeübt werden, wenn im Falle ihrer Berücksichtigung eine Mitteilungspflicht nach § 21 Abs. 1 bestünde.

2 cannot be exercised if a duty to report pursuant to § 21 para. 1 would exist in the event of their consideration.

§ 24 Mitteilung durch Konzernunternehmen

Gehört der Meldepflichtige zu einem Konzern, für den nach den §§ 290, 340i des Handelsgesetzbuchs ein Konzernabschluß aufgestellt werden muß, so können die Mitteilungspflichten nach § 21 Abs. 1 durch das Mutterunternehmen oder, wenn das Mutterunternehmen selbst ein Tochterunternehmen ist, durch dessen Mutterunternehmen erfüllt werden.

§ 24 Reporting by Group Companies

If the party under a duty to report belongs to a group for which a group financial report must be produced pursuant to §§ 290, 340i of the Commercial Code, then the duties to report pursuant to § 21 para. 1 can be performed by the parent company or, if the parent company is itself a subsidiary, by its parent company.

§ 25 Veröffentlichungspflichten der börsennotierten Gesellschaft

(1) Die börsennotierte Gesellschaft hat Mitteilungen nach § 21 Abs. 1 unverzüglich, spätestens neun Kalendertage nach Zugang der Mitteilung, in deutscher Sprache in einem überregionalen Börsenpflichtblatt zu veröffentlichen. In der Veröffentlichung ist der Meldepflichtige mit Name oder Firma und Wohnort oder Sitz anzugeben. Die börsennotierte Gesellschaft hat im Bundesanzeiger unverzüglich bekanntzumachen, in welchem Börsenpflichtblatt die Mitteilung veröffentlicht worden ist.

§ 25 Publication Duties of the Exchange-quoted Company

(1) The company quoted on the stock exchange shall publicize reports pursuant to § 21 para. 1 without delay, at the latest 9 calendar days after receipt of the report, in the German language in an official national stock exchange journal. The party under a duty to report is to be identified in the publication by name or firm name and residence or domicile. The company quoted on the stock exchange shall announce in the Federal Gazette without delay the official stock exchange journal in which the report has been published.

(2) Sind die Aktien der börsennotierten Gesellschaft an einer Börse in einem anderen Mitgliedstaat der Europäischen Gemeinschaften oder in einem anderen Vertragsstaat des Abkommens über den Europäischen Wirtschaftsraum zum amtlichen Handel zugelassen, so hat die Gesellschaft die Veröffentlichung nach Ab-

(2) If the stocks of the stock exchange-quoted company are admitted to official trading on a stock exchange in another member state of the European Communities or in another contracting state to the European Economic Area Agreement, then the company shall undertake publication pursuant to para. 1 sentences 1 and 2

satz 1 Satz 1 und 2 unverzüglich, spätestens neun Kalendertage nach Zugang der Mitteilung, auch in einem Börsenpflichtblatt dieses Staates oder, sofern das Recht dieses Staates eine andere Form der Unterrichtung des Publikums vorschreibt, in dieser anderen Form vorzunehmen. Die Veröffentlichung muß in einer Sprache abgefaßt werden, die in diesem Staat für solche Veröffentlichungen zugelassen ist.

(3) Die börsennotierte Gesellschaft hat dem Bundesaufsichtsamt unverzüglich einen Beleg über die Veröffentlichung nach den Absätzen 1 und 2 zu übersenden. Das Bundesaufsichtsamt unterrichtet die in Absatz 2 genannten Börsen über die Veröffentlichung.

(4) Das Bundesaufsichtsamt befreit auf schriftlichen Antrag die börsennotierte Gesellschaft von den Veröffentlichungspflichten nach den Absätzen 1 und 2, wenn es nach Abwägung der Umstände der Auffassung ist, daß die Veröffentlichung dem öffentlichen Interesse zuwiderlaufen oder der Gesellschaft erheblichen Schaden zufügen würde, sofern im letzteren Fall die Nichtveröffentlichung nicht zu einem Irrtum des Publikums über die für die Beurteilung der betreffenden Wertpapiere wesentlichen Tatsachen und Umstände führen kann.

§ 26 Veröffentlichungspflichten von Gesellschaften mit Sitz im Ausland

(1) Erreicht, übersteigt oder unterschreitet der Stimmrechtsanteil des Aktionärs einer Gesellschaft mit Sitz im Ausland, deren Aktien zum amtlichen Handel an einer inländischen Börse zugelassen sind, die in § 21

without delay, at the latest 9 calendar days after receipt of the report also in a stock exchange official journal of such country or, to the extent that the law of such country prescribes another form of informing the public, in such other form. The publication must be in a language which is permissible in such state for such publications.

(3) The stock exchange-quoted company shall send the Federal Supervisory Agency proof of publication pursuant to paras. 1 and 2 without delay. The Federal Supervisory Agency shall inform the stock exchanges specified in para. 2 of the publication.

(4) The Federal Supervisory Agency shall, upon written application, exempt the stock exchange-quoted company from the duties to publicize pursuant to paras. 1 and 2 if the Agency is, after consideration of the circumstances, of the opinion that the publication would disserve the public interest or would inflict substantial damage upon the company to the extent, in the latter event, that non-publication could not lead to misleading of the public concerning assessment of the essential facts and circumstances of the concerned securities.

§ 26 Publication Duties of Companies Domiciled Abroad

(1) If the voting rights share of the stockholder of a foreign domiciled company whose stocks are admitted to official trading on a domestic stock exchange reach, exceed or fall below the thresholds specified in § 21 para. 1

Abs. 1 Satz 1 genannten Schwellen, so ist die Gesellschaft, sofern nicht die Voraussetzungen des Absatzes 3 vorliegen, verpflichtet, diese Tatsache sowie die Höhe des Stimmrechtsanteils des Aktionärs unverzüglich, spätestens innerhalb von neun Kalendertagen, in einem überregionalen Börsenpflichtblatt zu veröffentlichen. Die Frist beginnt mit dem Zeitpunkt, zu dem die Gesellschaft Kenntnis hat, daß der Stimmrechtsanteil des Aktionärs die in § 21 Abs. 1 Satz 1 genannten Schwellen erreicht, überschreitet oder unterschreitet.

(2) Auf die Veröffentlichungen nach Absatz 1 ist § 25 Abs. 1 Satz 2 und 3, Abs. 3 und 4 entsprechend anzuwenden.

(3) Gesellschaften mit Sitz in einem anderen Mitgliedstaat der Europäischen Gemeinschaften oder in einem anderen Vertragsstaat des Abkommens über den Europäischen Wirtschaftsraum, deren Aktien sowohl an einer Börse im Sitzstaat als auch an einer inländischen Börse zum amtlichen Handel zugelassen sind, müssen Veröffentlichungen, die das Recht des Sitzstaates aufgrund des Artikels 10 der Richtlinie 88/627/EWG des Rates vom 12. Dezember 1988 über die bei Erwerb und Veräußerung einer bedeutenden Beteiligung an einer börsennotierten Gesellschaft zu veröffentlichenden Informationen (ABl. EG Nr. L 348 S. 62) vorschreibt, im Inland in einem überregionalen Börsenpflichtblatt in deutscher Sprache vornehmen. § 25 Abs. 1 Satz 3 gilt entsprechend.

§ 27 Nachweis mitgeteilter Beteiligungen

Wer eine Mitteilung nach § 21 Abs. 1 abgegeben hat, muß auf Verlangen des

sentence 1, then the company is bound, to the extent that the preconditions of para. 3 are not present, to publicize this fact and the extent of the voting rights share of the stockholder without delay, at the latest within 9 calendar days, in an official national stock exchange journal. The notice period begins at the point in time at which the company has knowledge that the voting rights share of the stockholder has reached, exceeded or fallen below the thresholds specified in § 21 para. 1 sentence 1.

(2) § 25 para. 1 sentences 2 and 3, paras. 3 and 4 respectively shall be applied to publications pursuant to para. 1.

(3) Companies domiciled in another member state of the European Communities or in another contracting state to the European Economic Area Agreement and whose stocks are admitted on a stock exchange in the domiciliary state as well as on a domestic stock exchange to official trading must undertake publications prescribed by the law of the domiciliary state on the basis of Council Directive 88/627/EC of December 12, 1988, Article 10, concerning information to be publicized upon acquisition and sale of a substantial equity holding in a stock exchange-quoted company (Off. Jr. EC No. L 348 p. 62) domestically in a national stock exchange reporting journal in the German language. § 25 para. 1 sentence 3 applies respectively.

§ 27 Evidence of Reported Equity Holdings

Whoever has submitted a report pursuant to § 21 para. 1 must, upon

Bundesaufsichtsamtes oder der börsennotierten Gesellschaft das Bestehen der mitgeteilten Beteiligung nachweisen.

demand of the Federal Supervisory Agency or of the stock exchange-quoted company, prove the existence of the reported equity holding.

§ 28 Ruhen des Stimmrechts

Stimmrechte aus Aktien, die einem Meldepflichtigen oder einem von ihm unmittelbar oder mittelbar kontrollierten Unternehmen zustehen, dürfen für die Zeit, für welche die Mitteilungspflichten nach § 21 Abs. 1 nicht erfüllt werden, nicht ausgeübt werden.

§ 28 Suspension of Voting Rights

Voting rights arising out of stocks belonging to a party under a duty to report or to an enterprise directly or indirectly controlled by such party may not be exercised for the time during which reporting duties pursuant to § 21 para. 1 are not performed.

§ 29 Befugnisse des Bundesaufsichtsamtes

(1) Das Bundesaufsichtsamt kann von der börsennotierten Gesellschaft und deren Aktionären Auskünfte und die Vorlage von Unterlagen verlangen, soweit dies zur Überwachung der Einhaltung der in diesem Abschnitt geregelten Pflichten erforderlich ist. Die Befugnisse nach Satz 1 bestehen auch gegenüber Personen und Unternehmen, deren Stimmrechte nach § 22 Abs. 1 zuzurechnen sind. § 16 Abs. 6 ist anzuwenden.

(2) Das Bundesaufsichtsamt kann Richtlinien aufstellen, nach denen es für den Regelfall beurteilt, ob die Voraussetzungen für einen mitteilungspflichtigen Vorgang oder eine Befreiung von den Mitteilungspflichten nach § 21 Abs. 1 gegeben sind. Die Richtlinien sind im Bundesanzeiger zu veröffentlichen.

(3) Das Bundesaufsichtsamt kann die Veröffentlichungen nach § 25 Abs. 1 und 2 auf Kosten der börsennotierten Gesellschaft vornehmen, wenn die Gesellschaft die Veröffentlichungspflicht nicht, nicht richtig, nicht voll-

§ 29 Federal Supervisory Agency Powers

(1) The Federal Supervisory Agency can demand information and the submission of documents of the stock exchange-quoted company and of its stockholders to the extent that this is necessary to supervise the performance of the duties regulated in this Part. The powers pursuant to sentence 1 are in effect also in respect to persons and enterprises whose voting rights are to be ascribed pursuant to § 22 para. 1. § 16 para. 6 shall be applied.

(2) The Federal Supervisory Agency can issue guidelines according to which it decides in a normal case whether the preconditions for a reportable event under the duty to report or whether an exemption from the duties to report pursuant to § 21 para. 1 are present. The guidelines shall be published in the Federal Gazette.

(3) The Federal Supervisory Agency can perform publications pursuant to § 25 paras. 1 and 2 at the cost of the stock exchange-quoted company if the company does not perform its duty to publicize or performs such

ständig oder nicht in der vorgeschriebenen Form erfüllt.

§ 30 Zusammenarbeit mit zuständigen Stellen im Ausland

(1) Das Bundesaufsichtsamt arbeitet mit den zuständigen Stellen der anderen Mitgliedstaaten der Europäischen Gemeinschaften, der anderen Vertragsstaaten des Abkommens über den Europäischen Wirtschaftsraum sowie in den Fällen der Nummern 1 und 4 auch mit den entsprechenden Stellen von Drittstaaten zusammen, um insbesondere darauf hinzuwirken, daß

1. Meldepflichtige mit Wohnsitz, Sitz oder gewöhnlichem Aufenthalt in einem dieser Staaten ihre Mitteilungspflichten ordnungsmäßig erfüllen,

2. börsennotierte Gesellschaften ihre Veröffentlichungspflicht nach § 25 Abs. 2 ordnungsmäßig erfüllen,

3. die nach den Vorschriften eines anderen Mitgliedstaates der Europäischen Gemeinschaften oder eines anderen Vertragsstaates des Abkommens über den Europäischen Wirtschaftsraum in diesem Staat Meldepflichtigen mit Wohnsitz, Sitz oder gewöhnlichem Aufenthalt im Inland ihre Mitteilungspflichten ordnungsmäßig erfüllen,

4. Gesellschaften mit Sitz im Ausland, deren Aktien an einer inländischen Börse zum amtlichen Handel zugelassen sind, ihre Veröffentlichungspflichten im Inland ordnungsmäßig erfüllen.

(2) Das Bundesaufsichtsamt darf den zuständigen Stellen der anderen Mitgliedstaaten oder Vertragsstaaten Tat-

duty improperly, incompletely or not in the prescribed form.

§ 30 Cooperation with the Responsible Foreign Offices

(1) The Federal Supervisory Agency shall cooperate with the responsible offices of the other member states of the European Communities, of the other contracting states to the European Economic Area Agreement and, in the event of nos. 1 and 4, also with the appropriate authorities of third countries, in order especially to further that

1. parties under a duty to report officially residing, domiciled or usually resident in one of these countries perform their duties to report in an orderly manner,

2. stock exchange-quoted companies perform their duty to publicize pursuant to § 25 para. 2 in an orderly manner,

3. the parties under a duty, pursuant to the regulations of another member state of the European Communities or of another contracting state to the European Economic Area Agreement, to report in such country and with a domestic official residence, domestically domiciled or usually domestically residing perform their duties to report in an orderly manner,

4. foreign domiciled companies whose stocks are admitted to official trading on a domestic stock exchange perform their duties to publicize domestically in an orderly manner.

(2) The Federal Supervisory Agency may communicate facts, including information pertaining to specific in-

sachen einschließlich personenbezogener Daten übermitteln, soweit dies zur Überwachung der Einhaltung der Mitteilungs- und Veröffentlichungspflichten erforderlich ist. Bei der Übermittlung ist darauf hinzuweisen, daß die zuständigen Stellen, unbeschadet ihrer Verpflichtungen in strafrechtlichen Angelegenheiten, die Verstöße gegen Mitteilungs- oder Veröffentlichungspflichten zum Gegenstand haben, die ihnen übermittelten Tatsachen einschließlich personenbezogener Daten ausschließlich zur Überwachung der Einhaltung dieser Pflichten oder im Rahmen damit zusammenhängender Verwaltungs- oder Gerichtsverfahren verwenden dürfen.

(3) Dem Bundesaufsichtsamt stehen im Fall des Absatzes 1 Nr. 3 die Befugnisse nach § 29 Abs. 1 zu.

Abschnitt 5: Verhaltensregeln für Wertpapierdienstleistungsunternehmen

§ 31 Allgemeine Verhaltensregeln

(1) Ein Wertpapierdienstleistungsunternehmen ist verpflichtet,

1. Wertpapierdienstleistungen mit der erforderlichen Sachkenntnis, Sorgfalt und Gewissenhaftigkeit im Interesse seiner Kunden zu erbringen,

2. sich um die Vermeidung von Interessenkonflikten zu bemühen und dafür zu sorgen, daß bei unvermeidbaren Interessenkonflikten der Kundenauftrag unter der gebotenen Wahrung des Kundeninteresses ausgeführt wird.

(2) Es ist ferner verpflichtet,

dividuals, to the responsible authorities of the other member states or contracting states to the extent that this is necessary to supervise observance of reporting and publication duties. In communicating facts, notice shall be given that the responsible authorities, without prejudice to their duties in criminal law matters concerning violations of reporting or publication duties, shall use the facts communicated to them (including information pertaining to specific individuals) exclusively to supervise observance of such duties or within the context of administrative or court proceedings in conjunction therewith.

(3) In the event of para. 1 no. 3, the Federal Supervisory Agency enjoys powers pursuant to § 29 para. 1.

Part five: Rules of Conduct for Securities Firms

§ 31 General Rules of Conduct

(1) A securities firm is obliged

1. to perform securities services with the necessary expert knowledge, care and conscientiousness in the interest of its customers,

2. to make an effort to avoid conflicts of interest and to take care that a customer order, in the event of unavoidable conflicts of interest, is performed with the requisite observance of the customer's interest.

(2) Such securities firm is additionally obliged

1. von seinen Kunden Angaben über ihre Erfahrungen oder Kenntnisse in Geschäften, die Gegenstand von Wertpapierdienstleistungen sein sollen, über ihre mit den Geschäften verfolgten Ziele und über ihre finanziellen Verhältnisse zu verlangen,

2. seinen Kunden alle zweckdienlichen Informationen mitzuteilen,

soweit dies zur Wahrung der Interessen der Kunden und im Hinblick auf Art und Umfang der beabsichtigten Geschäfte erforderlich ist.

(3) Die Absätze 1 und 2 gelten auch für Unternehmen mit Sitz im Ausland, die Wertpapierdienstleistungen gegenüber Kunden erbringen, die ihren gewöhnlichen Aufenthalt oder ihre Geschäftsleitung im Inland haben, sofern nicht die Wertpapierdienstleistung einschließlich der damit im Zusammenhang stehenden Nebenleistungen ausschließlich im Ausland erbracht wird.

§ 32 Besondere Verhaltensregeln

(1) Einem Wertpapierdienstleistungsunternehmen oder einem mit ihm verbundenen Unternehmen ist es verboten,

1. Kunden des Wertpapierdienstleistungsunternehmens den Ankauf oder Verkauf von Wertpapieren oder Derivaten zu empfehlen, wenn und soweit die Empfehlung nicht mit den Interessen der Kunden übereinstimmt;

2. Kunden des Wertpapierdienstleistungsunternehmens den Ankauf oder Verkauf von Wertpapieren oder Derivaten zu dem Zweck zu empfehlen, für Eigengeschäfte des

1. to demand of its customers information as to their experiences or knowledge in transactions contemplated by securities services, to demand information concerning the goals pursued by the transactions and concerning the customers' financial states,

2. to inform its customers of all useful information,

to the extent that this is necessary for protecting the interests of the customers and in reference to type and extent of the intended transactions.

(3) Paras. 1 and 2 apply also to enterprises domiciled abroad which render securities services to customers who have their usual residence or their business management domestically, to the extent that securities service including secondary services in conjunction therewith is not rendered exclusively abroad.

§ 32 Special Rules of Conduct

(1) A securities firm or an enterprise affiliated with such is barred from

1. recommending the purchase or the sale of securities or derivatives to customers of the securities firm, if and to the extent that the recommendation is not in the interests of the customers;

2. recommending the purchase or sale of securities or derivatives to customers of the securities firm with the goal of influencing prices in a particular direction for the

Wertpapierdienstleistungsunternehmens oder eines mit ihm verbundenen Unternehmens Preise in eine bestimmte Richtung zu lenken;

3. Eigengeschäfte aufgrund der Kenntnis von einem Auftrag eines Kunden des Wertpapierdienstleistungsunternehmens zum Ankauf oder Verkauf von Wertpapieren oder Derivaten abzuschließen, die Nachteile für den Auftraggeber zur Folge haben können.

(2) Den Geschäftsinhabern eines in der Rechtsform des Einzelkaufmanns betriebenen Wertpapierdienstleistungsunternehmens, bei anderen Wertpapierdienstleistungsunternehmen den Personen, die nach Gesetz oder Gesellschaftsvertrag mit der Führung der Geschäfte des Unternehmens betraut und zu seiner Vertretung ermächtigt sind, sowie den Angestellten eines Wertpapierdienstleistungsunternehmens, die mit der Durchführung von Geschäften in Wertpapieren oder Derivaten, der Wertpapieranalyse oder der Anlageberatung betraut sind, ist es verboten,

1. Kunden des Wertpapierdienstleistungsunternehmens den Ankauf oder Verkauf von Wertpapieren oder Derivaten unter den Voraussetzungen des Absatzes 1 Nr. 1 oder zu dem Zweck zu empfehlen, für den Abschluß von Geschäften für sich oder Dritte Preise von Wertpapieren oder Derivaten in eine bestimmte Richtung zu lenken;

2. aufgrund der Kenntnis von einem Auftrag eines Kunden des Wertpapierdienstleistungsunternehmens zum Ankauf oder Verkauf von Wertpapieren oder Derivaten Ge-

securities firm's own transactions or for an affiliated enterprise's own transactions;

3. executing transactions for its own account on the basis of knowledge of an order of a customer of the securities firm for the purchase or sale of securities or derivatives which could result in disadvantages for the order giver.

(2) The proprietors of a securities firm operated in the legal form of a sole proprietorship or, in the case of other securities firms the persons, pursuant to law or articles of incorporation, entrusted with the management of the enterprise's business and authorized to represent such enterprise, and the employees of a securities firm entrusted with the execution of transactions in securities or derivatives or with the analysis of securities or with investment consulting are barred from

1. recommending the purchase or sale of securities or derivatives to customers of the securities firm under preconditions of para. 1 no. 1 or with the purpose of influencing prices of securities or derivatives in a particular direction for the execution of transactions for themselves or for third persons;

2. executing transactions for themselves or for a third party on the basis of knowledge of an order of a customer of the securities firm to purchase or sell securities or

schäfte für sich oder einen Dritten abzuschließen, die Nachteile für den Auftraggeber zur Folge haben können.

(3) Die Absätze 1 und 2 gelten unter den in § 31 Abs. 3 bestimmten Voraussetzungen auch für Unternehmen mit Sitz im Ausland.

§ 33 Organisationspflichten

Ein Wertpapierdienstleistungsunternehmen

1. ist verpflichtet, die für eine ordnungsmäßige Durchführung der Wertpapierdienstleistung notwendigen Mittel und Verfahren vorzuhalten und wirksam einzusetzen;

2. muß so organisiert sein, daß bei der Erbringung der Wertpapierdienstleistung Interessenkonflikte zwischen dem Wertpapierdienstleistungsunternehmen und seinen Kunden oder Interessenkonflikte zwischen verschiedenen Kunden des Wertpapierdienstleistungsunternehmens möglichst gering sind;

3. muß über angemessene interne Kontrollverfahren verfügen, die geeignet sind, Verstößen gegen Verpflichtungen nach diesem Gesetz entgegenzuwirken.

§ 34 Aufzeichnungs- und Aufbewahrungspflichten

(1) Ein Wertpapierdienstleistungsunternehmen ist verpflichtet,

1. bei der Erbringung von Wertpapierdienstleistungen den Auftrag und hierzu erteilte Anweisungen des Kunden sowie die Ausführung des Auftrags und

derivatives, which transactions could result in disadvantages for the order giver.

(3) Under the preconditions specified in § 31 para. 3, paras. 1 and 2 also apply to foreign domiciled enterprises.

§ 33 Organizational Duties

A securities firm

1. is obliged to maintain the means and procedures necessary for orderly performance of securities service and to employ them effectively;

2. must be organized in such a way so that in performing securities service, conflicts of interest between the securities firm and its customers or conflicts of interest between different customers of the securities firm are minimized to the fullest extent possible;

3. must have appropriate internal control procedures suitable for counteracting violations of duties pursuant to this Act.

§ 34 Recording and Record-keeping Duties

(1) A securities firm is obliged to record

1. the order and associated instructions of the customer in performing securities services and to record the performance of the order and

2. den Namen des Angestellten, der den Auftrag des Kunden angenommen hat, sowie die Uhrzeit der Erteilung und Ausführung des Auftrags

aufzuzeichnen.

(2) Das Bundesministerium der Finanzen kann nach Anhörung der Deutschen Bundesbank durch Rechtsverordnung, die nicht der Zustimmung des Bundesrates bedarf, die Wertpapierdienstleistungsunternehmen zu weiteren Aufzeichnungen verpflichten, soweit diese zur Überwachung der Verpflichtungen der Wertpapierdienstleistungsunternehmen durch das Bundesaufsichtsamt erforderlich sind. Das Bundesministerium der Finanzen kann die Ermächtigung durch Rechtsverordnung auf das Bundesaufsichtsamt übertragen.

(3) Die Aufzeichnungen nach den Absätzen 1 und 2 sind mindestens sechs Jahre aufzubewahren. Für die Aufbewahrung gilt § 257 Abs. 3 und 5 des Handelsgesetzbuchs entsprechend.

§ 35 Überwachung der Verhaltensregeln

(1) Das Bundesaufsichtsamt kann, soweit dies zur Überwachung der Einhaltung der in diesem Abschnitt geregelten Pflichten erforderlich ist, von den Wertpapierdienstleistungsunternehmen, den mit diesen verbundenen Unternehmen und den in § 32 Abs. 2 genannten Personen Auskünfte und die Vorlage von Unterlagen verlangen. § 16 Abs. 6 ist anzuwenden. Während der üblichen Arbeitszeit ist den Bediensteten des Bundesaufsichtsamtes, soweit dies zur Wahrnehmung seiner Aufgaben nach diesem Abschnitt erforderlich ist, das Betreten der

2. the name of the employee who has taken the customer's order as well as the day and time of day of the receipt and of the performance of the order.

(2) The Federal Finance Ministry can, after hearing the German Bundesbank, require additional recording from the securities firms by administrative rule that does not require the consent of the Federal Senate, to the extent that the Federal Supervisory Agency requires such rule for supervising the duties of the securities firms. The Federal Finance Ministry can delegate such authority to the Federal Supervisory Agency by administrative rule.

(3) The records pursuant to paras. 1 and 2 shall be kept for at least six years. Commercial Code § 257 paras. 3 and 5 apply respectively to such record-keeping.

§ 35 Supervising Rules of Conduct

(1) The Federal Supervisory Agency can, to the extent necessary for supervising the observance of the duties regulated in this Part, demand of the securities firms and of their affiliated enterprises and of the persons described in § 32 para. 2 information and the submission of documents. § 16 para. 6 shall be applied. Entrance to the real estate and business offices of the securities firms and of the enterprises affiliated with such firms is to be allowed during normal working hours to the employees of the Federal Supervisory Agency to the extent that

Grundstücke und Geschäftsräume der Wertpapierdienstleistungsunternehmen und der mit diesen verbundenen Unternehmen zu gestatten.

(2) Das Bundesaufsichtsamt kann Richtlinien aufstellen, nach denen es für den Regelfall beurteilt, ob die Anforderungen nach den §§ 31 bis 33 erfüllt sind. Die Deutsche Bundesbank, das Bundesaufsichtsamt für das Kreditwesen sowie die Spitzenverbände der betroffenen Wirtschaftskreise sind vor dem Erlaß der Richtlinien anzuhören; Richtlinien zu § 33 sind im Einvernehmen mit dem Bundesaufsichtsamt für das Kreditwesen zu erlassen. Die Richtlinien sind im Bundesanzeiger zu veröffentlichen.

§ 36 Prüfung der Meldepflichten und Verhaltensregeln

(1) Das Bundesaufsichtsamt hat bei Wertpapierdienstleistungsunternehmen die Einhaltung der Meldepflichten nach § 9 und der in diesem Abschnitt geregelten Pflichten in der Regel einmal jährlich zu prüfen. Bei den in § 2 Abs. 4 Nr. 1 genannten Kreditinstituten und Zweigstellen soll die Prüfung in der Regel zusammen mit der Depotprüfung nach § 30 des Gesetzes über das Kreditwesen durch den Depotprüfer erfolgen. Dem Bundesaufsichtsamt für das Kreditwesen ist eine Ausfertigung des Prüfungsberichts zu übermitteln.

(2) Das Bundesministerium der Finanzen kann durch Rechtsverordnung, die nicht der Zustimmung des Bundesrates bedarf, nähere Bestimmungen über Art, Umfang und Zeitpunkt der Prüfung nach Absatz 1 erlassen, soweit dies zur Erfüllung der Aufgaben des Bundesaufsichtsamtes

this is necessary for the performance of its tasks pursuant to this Part.

(2) The Federal Supervisory Agency can issue guidelines according to which the Agency shall judge, in a normal case, whether the requirements pursuant to §§ 31 to 33 have been met. The German Bundesbank, the Federal Banking Supervisory Agency and the leading associations of the concerned business circles shall be heard before the guidelines are issued; guidelines pertaining to § 33 shall be issued in agreement with the Federal Banking Supervisory Agency. The guidelines shall be published in the Federal Gazette.

§ 36 Auditing Reporting Duties and Rules of Conduct

(1) The Federal Supervisory Agency shall, as a rule, audit securities firms regarding the observance of reporting duties pursuant to § 9 and the duties regulated in this Part once yearly. In the case of the credit institutions and branches specified in § 2 para. 4 no. 1, the audit, as a rule, should take place together with the custody deposit audit pursuant to § 30 of the Banking Act. The Federal Banking Supervisory Agency shall be supplied with a copy of the audit report.

(2) The Federal Finance Ministry can promulgate further particulars as to type, extent and point in time of the audit pursuant to para. 1 by administrative rule which does not require the consent of the Federal Senate, especially to counteract undesirable states of affairs in securities and deriv-

erforderlich ist, insbesondere um Mißständen im Handel mit Wertpapieren und Derivaten entgegenzuwirken, um auf die Einhaltung der Meldepflichten nach § 9 und der in diesem Abschnitt geregelten Pflichten hinzuwirken und um zu diesem Zweck einheitliche Unterlagen zu erhalten. Das Bundesministerium der Finanzen kann die Ermächtigung durch Rechtsverordnung auf das Bundesaufsichtsamt übertragen.

atives trading, in order to further the performance of reporting duties pursuant to § 9 and the duties regulated in this Part and the receipt of uniform documents to this purpose. The Federal Finance Ministry can delegate the authority by administrative rule to the Federal Supervisory Agency.

§ 37 Ausnahmen

(1) Die Verpflichtungen nach den §§ 31 bis 34 gelten nicht für

1. Unternehmen, die Wertpapierdienstleistungen ausschließlich für ihr Mutterunternehmen oder ihre Tochterunternehmen im Sinne des § 1 Abs. 6 und 7 des Gesetzes über das Kreditwesen oder andere Tochterunternehmen ihres Mutterunternehmens erbringen;

2. die öffentliche Schuldenverwaltung des Bundes, eines seiner Sondervermögen, eines Landes, eines anderen Mitgliedstaates der Europäischen Gemeinschaften oder eines anderen Vertragsstaates des Abkommens über den Europäischen Wirtschaftsraum, die Deutsche Bundesbank sowie die Zentralbanken der anderen Mitgliedstaaten oder Vertragsstaaten.

(2) Die §§ 31, 32 und 34 gelten nicht für Geschäfte, die an einer Börse zwischen zwei Wertpapierdienstleistungsunternehmen abgeschlossen werden. Wertpapierdienstleistungsunternehmen, die an einer Börse ein Geschäft als Kommissionär abschließen, unterliegen insoweit den Pflich-

§ 37 Exceptions

(1) The duties pursuant to §§ 31 to 34 do not apply

1. to enterprises which perform securities services exclusively for their parent companies or for their subsidiaries within the meaning of § 1 paras. 6 and 7 of the Banking Act or for other subsidiaries of their parent company.

2. to public debt administration of the Federal Government, of one of its special assets, of a state [Land], of another member state of the European Communities or of another contracting state to the European Economic Area Agreement, to the German Bundesbank or to the central banks of the other member states or contracting states.

(2) §§ 31, 32 and 34 do not apply to transactions which are executed on a stock exchange between two securities firms. Securities firms which execute a transaction on a stock exchange as commission agent are, to that extent, subject to the duties pursuant to § 34. § 33 does not apply

ten nach § 34. § 33 gilt nicht für ein Wertpapierdienstleistungsunternehmen, das ausschließlich Geschäfte betreibt, die in Satz 1 genannt sind.

to a securities firm which exclusively performs transactions which are specified in sentence 1.

Abschnitt 6: Straf- und Bußgeldvorschriften

Part six: Criminal and Monetary Penalty Regulations

§ 38 Strafvorschriften

(1) Mit Freiheitsstrafe bis zu fünf Jahren oder mit Geldstrafe wird bestraft, wer

1. entgegen einem Verbot nach § 14 Abs. 1 Nr. 1 oder Abs. 2 ein Insiderpapier erwirbt oder veräußert,

2. entgegen einem Verbot nach § 14 Abs. 1 Nr. 2 eine Insidertatsache mitteilt oder zugänglich macht oder

3. entgegen einem Verbot nach § 14 Abs. 1 Nr. 3 den Erwerb oder die Veräußerung eines Insiderpapiers empfiehlt.

(2) Einem Verbot im Sinne des Absatzes 1 steht ein entsprechendes ausländisches Verbot gleich.

§ 38 Criminal Regulations

(1) A prison sentence of up to five years or a monetary penalty shall be imposed upon whoever

1. acquires or sells an insider security in violation of the bar pursuant to § 14 para. 1 no. 1 or para. 2,

2. reports or renders accessible an insider fact in violation of a bar pursuant to § 14 para. 1 no. 2 or

3. recommends the acquisition or the sale of an insider security in violation of a bar pursuant to § 14 para. 1 no. 3.

(2) A respective foreign bar shall be deemed the equivalent of a bar within the meaning of para. 1.

§ 39 Bußgeldvorschriften

(1) Ordnungswidrig handelt, wer vorsätzlich oder leichtfertig

1. entgegen

a) § 9 Abs. 1 Satz 1, 2 oder 3 jeweils in Verbindung mit Absatz 2, auch in Verbindung mit einer Rechtsverordnung nach Absatz 3,

b) § 15 Abs. 2 Satz 1 oder

c) § 21 Abs. 1 Satz 1, auch in Verbindung mit § 22 Abs. 1 oder 2,

§ 39 Monetary Penalty Regulations

(1) It is a misdemeanor to intentionally or carelessly

1. in violation of

a) § 9 para. 1 sentence 1, 2 or 3 respectively in conjunction with para. 2 also in conjunction with an administrative rule pursuant to para. 3

b) § 15 para. 2 sentence 1 or

c) § 21 para. 1 sentence 1 also in conjunction with § 22 para. 1 or 2,

eine Mitteilung nicht, nicht richtig, nicht vollständig, nicht in der vorgeschriebenen Form oder nicht rechtzeitig macht,

2. entgegen

a) § 15 Abs. 1 Satz 1 in Verbindung mit Abs. 3 Satz 1 oder

b) § 25 Abs. 1 Satz 1 in Verbindung mit Satz 2, § 25 Abs. 2 Satz 1 in Verbindung mit Satz 2 oder § 26 Abs. 1 Satz 1

eine Veröffentlichung nicht, nicht richtig, nicht vollständig, nicht in der vorgeschriebenen Form oder nicht rechtzeitig vornimmt,

3. entgegen § 15 Abs. 3 Satz 2 eine Veröffentlichung vornimmt,

4. entgegen § 15 Abs. 3 Satz 3, auch in Verbindung mit Satz 5, oder § 25 Abs. 1 Satz 3, auch in Verbindung mit § 26 Abs. 3 Satz 2, eine Bekanntmachung nicht, nicht richtig oder nicht rechtzeitig vornimmt,

5. entgegen § 15 Abs. 4 oder § 25 Abs. 3 Satz 1, auch in Verbindung mit § 26 Abs. 2, eine Veröffentlichung oder einen Beleg nicht oder nicht rechtzeitig übersendet,

6. entgegen § 34 Abs. 1, auch in Verbindung mit einer Rechtsverordnung nach § 34 Abs. 2, eine Aufzeichnung nicht, nicht richtig oder nicht vollständig fertigt oder

7. entgegen § 34 Abs. 3 Satz 1 eine Aufzeichnung nicht oder nicht mindestens sechs Jahre aufbewahrt.

(2) Ordnungswidrig handelt, wer vorsätzlich oder fahrlässig

1. einer vollziehbaren Anordnung nach § 15 Abs. 5 Satz 1, § 16 Abs. 2, 3 Satz 1, Abs. 4 oder 5, § 29 Abs. 1,

fail to report, report improperly, report incompletely, report other than in the prescribed form or report not in due time,

2. in violation of

a) § 15 para. 1 sentence 1 in conjunction with para. 3 sentence 1 or

b) § 25 para. 1 sentence 1 in conjunction with sentence 2, § 25 para. 2 sentence 1 in conjunction with sentence 2 or § 26 para. 1 sentence 1

fail to publicize, publicize improperly, publicize incompletely, publicize other than in the prescribed form or publicize not in due time,

3. in violation of § 15 para. 3 sentence 2 perform publication,

4. in violation of § 15 para. 3 sentence 3 also in conjunction with sentence 5, or § 25 para. 1 sentence 3, also in conjunction with § 26 para. 3 sentence 2 fail to announce, announce improperly or announce not in due time,

5. in violation of § 15 para. 4 or § 25 para. 3 sentence 1, also in conjunction with § 26 para. 2 fail to send a publication or proof or fail to send such in due time,

6. in violation of § 34 para. 1, also in conjunction with an administrative rule pursuant to § 34 para. 2 fail to record, improperly record or incompletely record or

7. in violation of § 34 para. 3 sentence 1 to keep a record or to keep a record for at least 6 years.

(2) Whoever intentionally or negligently does the following commits a misdemeanor

1. acts contrary to an enforceable administrative order pursuant to § 15 para. 5 sentence 1, § 16 paras. 2, 3

auch in Verbindung mit § 30 Abs. 3, oder § 35 Abs. 1 Satz 1 zuwiderhandelt oder

2. ein Betreten entgegen § 15 Abs. 5 Satz 2, § 16 Abs. 3 Satz 2 oder § 35 Abs. 1 Satz 3 nicht gestattet oder entgegen § 16 Abs. 3 Satz 3 nicht duldet.

(3) Die Ordnungswidrigkeit kann in den Fällen des Absatzes 1 Nr. 2 Buchstabe a und Nr. 3 mit einer Geldbuße bis zu drei Millionen Deutsche Mark, in den Fällen des Absatzes 1 Nr. 1 Buchstabe b und c mit einer Geldbuße bis zu fünfhunderttausend Deutsche Mark, in den Fällen des Absatzes 1 Nr. 1 Buchstabe a, Nr. 2 Buchstabe b, Nr. 4 bis 7 sowie des Absatzes 2 mit einer Geldbuße bis zu einhunderttausend Deutsche Mark geahndet werden.

§ 40 Zuständige Verwaltungsbehörde

Verwaltungsbehörde im Sinne des § 36 Abs. 1 Nr. 1 des Gesetzes über Ordnungswidrigkeiten ist das Bundesaufsichtsamt für den Wertpapierhandel.

Abschnitt 7:
Übergangsbestimmungen

§ 41 Erstmalige Mitteilungs- und Veröffentlichungspflicht

(1) Mitteilungen nach § 9 Abs. 1 müssen erstmals zu dem Zeitpunkt abgegeben werden, der durch Rechtsverordnung des Bundesministeriums der Finanzen, die nicht der Zustimmung des Bundesrates bedarf, bestimmt wird; der Zeitpunkt darf nicht nach

sentence 1, para. 4 or 5, § 29 para. 1, also in conjunction with § 30 para. 3 or § 35 para. 1 sentence 1 or

2. does not allow entrance in violation of § 15 para. 5 sentence 2, § 16 para. 3 sentence 2 or § 35 para. 1 sentence 3 or in violation of § 16 para. 3 sentence 3 does not tolerate.

(3) The misdemeanor can be prosecuted in the event of para. 1 no. 2 letter a and no. 3 with a monetary penalty of up to 3 Million German Marks, and in the event of para. 1 no. 1 letters b and c with a monetary penalty of up to 500,000 German Marks, in the event of para. 1 no. 1 letter a, no. 2 letter b, nos. 4 to 7 as well as of para. 2 with a monetary penalty of up to 100,000 German Marks.

§ 40 Responsible Administrative Authority

The Federal Securities Trade Supervisory Agency is the administrative authority within the meaning of § 36 para. 1 no. 1 of the Misdemeanors Act.

Part seven:
Transitional Provisions

§ 41 Initial Reporting and Publication Duty

(1) Reports pursuant to § 9 para. 1 must initially be submitted at that point in time determined by administrative rule of the Federal Finance Ministry which does not require the consent of the Federal Senate; such point in time shall not be later than

dem 1. Januar 1996 liegen. § 9 Abs. 4 ist entsprechend anzuwenden.

(2) Wem am 1. Januar 1995 unter Berücksichtigung des § 22 Abs. 1 fünf Prozent oder mehr der Stimmrechte einer börsennotierten Gesellschaft zustehen, hat spätestens am Tag der ersten Hauptversammlung der Gesellschaft, die nach dem 1. April 1995 stattfindet, der Gesellschaft sowie dem Bundesaufsichtsamt die Höhe seines Anteils am stimmberechtigten Kapital unter Angabe seiner Anschrift schriftlich mitzuteilen, sofern nicht zu diesem Zeitpunkt bereits eine Mitteilung gemäß § 21 Abs. 1 abgegeben worden ist.

(3) Die Gesellschaft hat Mitteilungen nach Absatz 2 innerhalb von einem Monat nach Zugang nach Maßgabe des § 25 Abs. 1 Satz 1, Abs. 2 zu veröffentlichen und dem Bundesaufsichtsamt unverzüglich einen Beleg über die Veröffentlichung zu übersenden.

(4) Auf die Pflichten nach den Absätzen 2 und 3 sind die §§ 23, 24, 25 Abs. 1 Satz 3, Abs. 3 Satz 2, Abs. 4, §§ 27 bis 30 entsprechend anzuwenden.

(5) Ordnungswidrig handelt, wer vorsätzlich oder leichtfertig

1. entgegen Absatz 2 eine Mitteilung nicht, nicht richtig, nicht vollständig, nicht in der vorgeschriebenen Form oder nicht rechtzeitig macht oder

2. entgegen Absatz 3 in Verbindung mit § 25 Abs. 1 Satz 1 oder Abs. 2 eine Veröffentlichung nicht, nicht richtig, nicht vollständig, nicht in der vorgeschriebenen Form oder nicht rechtzeitig vornimmt oder einen Beleg nicht oder nicht rechtzeitig übersendet.

January 1, 1996. § 9 para. 4 shall be applied respectively.

(2) Whoever on January 1, 1995 has voting rights with respect to § 22 para. 1 to five percent or more of a stock exchange-quoted company shall, at the latest on the day of the first shareholders' meeting of the company which takes place after April 1, 1995, report to the company and to the Federal Supervisory Agency the amount of his or her share of the voting capital and including his or her address in writing to the extent that a report pursuant to § 21 para. 1 has not already been submitted by this point in time.

(3) The company shall publicize reports pursuant to para. 2 within one month after receipt pursuant to the measure of § 25 para. 1 sentence 1, para. 2 and shall send the Federal Supervisory Agency proof of publication without delay.

(4) §§ 23, 24, 25 para. 1 sentence 3, para. 3 sentence 2, para. 4, §§ 27 to 30 shall be applied respectively to the duties pursuant to paras. 2 and 3.

(5) Whoever intentionally or carelessly does the following shall commit a misdemeanor;

1. in violation of para. 2 does not report, improperly reports, reports incompletely, reports other than in the prescribed form or does not report in due time or

2. in violation of para. 3 in conjunction with § 25 para. 1 sentence 1 or para. 2 does not publicize, improperly publicizes, incompletely publicizes, publicizes other than in the prescribed form or does not publicize in due time or does not or does not in due time send proof.

53

(6) Die Ordnungswidrigkeit kann in den Fällen des Absatzes 5 Nr. 1 mit einer Geldbuße bis zu fünfhunderttausend Deutsche Mark und in den Fällen des Absatzes 5 Nr. 2 mit einer Geldbuße bis zu einhunderttausend Deutsche Mark geahndet werden.

(6) In the event of para. 5 no. 1, the misdemeanor can be punished with a monetary penalty of up to 500,000 German Marks and in the event of para. 5 no. 2 with a monetary penalty of up to 100,000 German Marks.

Schlagwortverzeichnis/Index

Fundstellenschlüssel: § und ggfs. Absatz
Cite key: § and, if appropriate, paragraph

Bitte beachten Sie
die nachfolgenden Verlagsanzeigen

Peltzer / Brooks

GmbH deutsch-englisch

German Law Pertaining to
Companies with Limited Liability

Synoptische Textausgabe mit einer ausführlichen englischen Einführung in das GmbH-Recht. Von RA und
Notar Dr. *Martin Peltzer* und WP *Jermyn P. Brooks*.
2. erneuerte Auflage 1987 mit Nachtrag 1993, 154 Seiten
DIN A 4, brosch. 68,– DM. ISBN 3 504 32534 8

Die Neuauflage berücksichtigt die Änderungen des
Bilanzrichtlinien-Gesetzes und des 2. Gesetzes zur
Bekämpfung der Wirtschaftskriminalität; in einem
Nachtrag sind Änderungen aus den Jahren 1990-1993
berücksichtigt. Dem Gesetzestext in beiden Sprachen
ist eine Darstellung des GmbH-Rechts in englischer
Sprache vorangestellt, mit der die Rechtsform der GmbH
erläutert sowie die Gesetzesänderungen beleuchtet
werden. Daneben enthält sie einen kurz gefaßten Führer
durch die die GmbH berührenden Steuer- und Bilan-
zierungsfragen.

Ein Mustergesellschaftsvertrag, ein Musteranstellungs-
vertrag mit einem GmbH-Geschäftsführer und ein
zweisprachiges Stichwortregister runden dieses Nach-
schlagebuch ab.

Verlag Dr. Otto Schmidt · Köln

Peltzer / Doyle / Allen

Handelsgesetzbuch
Deutsch-englische Textausgabe
German Commercial Code

Mit einer englischen Einleitung von RA und Notar Dr. *Martin Peltzer*, RA *Jonathan Doyle* und RAin *Marie-Thérèse Allen*. 3. überarbeitete Auflage 1995 in Vorbereitung, ca. 370 Seiten, ca. 130,– DM. ISBN 3 504 45503 9

Diese synoptisch aufgebaute zweisprachige Textausgabe des Handelsgesetzbuchs bietet sowohl für den deutschen als auch für den englischsprachigen Benutzer eine praktische Arbeitserleichterung und Übersetzungshilfe.

Auf eine bloße Wortlautübersetzung wurde zugunsten einer interpretierenden Darstellung verzichtet, was Verständnisschwierigkeiten englischsprachiger Leser gegenüber dem deutschen Recht nahezu ausschließt.

„... International tätige Anwaltskanzleien, Unternehmensberater, Wirtschaftsprüfer, Steuerberater sowie ausländische Kaufleute und ihre Berater werden auf dieses Werk gerne mit Gewinn zurückgreifen ...“
Rechtsanwalt Dr. Karl Heinz Weiss zur 2. Auflage
in „Recht der Internationalen Wirtschaft“ 6/94

Verlag Dr. Otto Schmidt · Köln